THE DANDELION PICKER

THE
DANDELION PICKER

PATRICIA PLOSS

PALMETTO
PUBLISHING
Charleston, SC
www.PalmettoPublishing.com

Copyright © 2024 by Patricia Ploss

Paperback ISBN: 979-8-8229-4125-0

DEDICATION

I thought to myself that writing the dedication for this book would be the easy part of writing the story! However, the more I thought about who this book would be dedicated to, the more I thought about all the people who have been involved in Dawson's progress and continue to be on many levels. Everyone from the person, who called 911 to report the accident, to the service providers who helped Dawson to move forward in healthy and positive ways. So, I must dedicate this book to the human spirit. That which leads us to lend a helping hand to those in need. That voice inside of us that prompts us to reach out to others. Dawson and I both wish that anyone who reads this book can find hope. Believe that right will overcome wrong, that there are blessings in every tragedy. Don't give up, and don't let go. This book is also dedicated to Dawson. His unfolding story that continues on after these words are read, will be his journey. As his mother, I pray for guidance and happiness for him. I thank him for letting me write the difficult things and the happy things. They are all blessings because he is alive today. I'm not standing over a lonely grave, or a hospital bed. I can hug him and tell him I love him to his face. Thankfulness is never ending.

CHAPTER 1

Life rarely happens as we expect it to. At least not in my experience so far! Sometimes when you aren't on the right track, God reaches down and puts you on a path to find the way to Him. The events and experiences I am going to tell you about, I originally believed were only about my son and how I perceived it all. I didn't realize for a long time that God was speaking to not only Dawson but to our family. When I understood that, I knew that this life lesson was to be shared. There are countless families going through very painful traumas, and I believe if we share with one another and lift each other up, we will find strength and common ground. This past year has affected our family in ways that have been life-changing. Faith has been tested; arguments have been made. Questions have been answered, and new ones have been asked. Growth has been painful, liberating, and also wonderful. The kindness of strangers that have become friends for life and those blessed with the gift of physical and spiritual healing have shown us that God truly loves us and wants us to be fulfilled with all life has to offer.

With that being said, you learn to understand that life isn't always an endless parade of excitement or tragedy. Sometimes years pass with nothing more notable than the celebrations of birthdays and holidays. The magic of Christmas or the truly special meaning of a birthday can become rote and routine, with just the number of candles on the cake or monetary gifts instead of toys under the tree as the kids grow up. The miracles that happen every day become unnoticed and taken for granted.

When things don't go as expected, your focus shifts, your habits change, and your direction becomes unclear and stressful. You question things you never thought of. You question God and wonder what you may have done to deserve such hardships. These negative thoughts tend to change your personality, your outlook, and sadly, your faith. After this very long year, everything has shifted once again. A year ago, Dawson was in a very dark place. As I write this, he is at a Wednesday night church service. His mind is clear from drugs and alcohol; his focus is a healthy future. Our family has had growing pains of facing our own past traumas and the willingness to let them go, heal, and move forward. We all are moving at our own pace. It's scary and frustrating. It also brings pure laughter and joy after so many months of gut-wrenching fear, pain, anger, and sadness.

Telling this story has been cathartic and also painful I am forever grateful to my close circle of friends who have supported us through what sometimes has felt like a never ending barrage of negativity. My friends are incredibly strong and I am truly blessed to have them in my life.

I thought I had raised my son to know right from wrong and all the things parents have told their children through the centuries. Yet somehow, things went wrong, and God allowed tragedy to enter our lives. He also brought us through it. There are things we are all meant to do—helping one another with the telling of our stories, reaching out to help other people, and giving the glory to God. This is how to move forward in this life to the one promised us in next.

It was summer 2004. I was a mom with a minivan. My son Dawson was five, and my daughter Rachel was four. We were driving on the country road from home, heading to town for groceries that day. My husband, Tony, was working, selling insurance at the time, and the kids and I had a long list of errands to run. I glanced into my rearview mirror and looked at my babies in their car seats. My heart was filled with love for them, as mothers' hearts are. They were looking out their windows at the surrounding fields of flowers and crops.

I smiled and asked them, "What are you two gonna be when you grow up?"

Rachel immediately answered, "I'm going to be a doctor, Mommy, and help people feel better!"

"That's a great idea, sweetheart! What about you, Dawson?"

He was looking out the window and thinking hard. Finally, he looked up into the mirror at me, with his big, brilliant blue eyes, and said, "I'm going to be a dandelion picker, Mommy! I'll pick the very best ones for you!"

Tears came to my eyes as his innocent face brightened with his thoughts. "That sounds super, honey. I love that you want to pick dandelions for me!"

The years passed, and the kids grew. Rachel sailed through school and took herself quite seriously. She had a few ups and downs, but nothing like Dawson did. She was always focused on a mission to be the very best she could at everything she did. She also looked out for the underdogs at school. She wouldn't let kids bully other kids.

We were called into school once when she was in the fifth grade. She'd stood up for a shy little girl and spoken her mind to the teacher. The teacher thought she was sassing her, and we were called in to discuss her attitude that they felt was disrespectful. In truth, she was defending this girl from the ones that were bullying her behind the teacher's back. Rachel was always strong that way.

Later on, she stood up for her big brother. It cost her entrance into the National Honor Society. When she took down the son of the basketball coach for calling her brother names, she was blackballed right out of NHS and told she had poor character. Rachel went on to be elected president of the Sunshine Club and VP of FFA.

She was selected to be on the town's tree committee. She earned her Girl Scout Gold Award at sixteen. She was crowned both 4H royalty and Miss Pulaski County 2018. She further showed her empathy toward people with her grand champion public speaking at the Indiana State Fair. Her speech encompassed all people and their struggles and how to believe in oneself. She has continued on into the philanthropy program at IUPUI. NHS lost a wonderful human being when they said she had poor character.

Dawson's story was much different than Rachel's. He had a tough road, way back from the start. Preschool was a huge struggle. He bounced off the walls, couldn't sit still to listen, couldn't concentrate on anything for very long and struggled to follow too many directions at once. Quickly the other kids shut him out. By the time he reached kindergarten, he was ostracized completely. Still, he tried to fit in, desperately tried to follow directions to make friends. No one would befriend him. So he clung to the teachers and office staff instead.

I wanted to take him to the doctor for testing to see if there was a problem but was told he was too young for a diagnosis. Kindergarten was so frustrating for him. We considered holding him back. Instead, we moved him from a first-year kindergarten teacher to a solid veteran teacher, who was better able to guide him through the second semester. It took until second grade to get the ADHD diagnosis. By then, he was becoming an introvert. We started him on meds, and he immediately turned himself around. But it was too late for him in the social aspect of school. He had no one to talk to or play with. He sought out teachers for friends.

At home, he played with Legos and watched TV. He was never invited to even one birthday party or play date. He was a very lonely little boy. Tony had gone from selling insurance to farming and tried to get Dawson interested in tractors and things. But Dawson didn't enjoy it at all. 4H was part of our lives then, and Rachel was interested in showing pigs. She and Tony got into that and even raising pigs for many years. Dawson showed a sheep his first year and then reluctantly agreed to show pigs. He didn't enjoy it at all. For a few years, the kids showed ducks as well. He agreed to do that, because he didn't have to work with it, like a pig, or a sheep. Finally, we got him to try shooting sports. He excelled at that, but he was never very excited about it. He met a girl who was also in shooting sports, and they decided they were boyfriend and girlfriend in the fifth grade. She went to a different school, so he rarely saw her.

This is one of my favorite photos of Dawson. His smile is so beautiful!

Dawson became quieter by middle school and didn't want to spend as much time with me as when he was younger. Rachel was doing her own things and drifting further away from Dawson. Tony and I tried to find things Dawson might be interested in, but other than Legos and video games, nothing seemed to pique his interest, just solitary activities. I knew he was hurting inside, and I tried to connect with him as I once did. We took advantage of the peer facilitator program at school for a few years. That meant a senior student would come to eat lunch with him and go to study hall or gym class. We thought that would help him to learn some social skills. It really didn't do much. It just made him feel even further separated from the other kids. The school never really did anything to help Dawson. They preferred to brush it under the rug and dismiss us. The school would just tell him to try harder at making friends. Dawson spent an entire month, eating his lunch in the restroom. Not one person noticed he was not in the cafeteria. When he finally told us this, we were devastated. He did have a couple of teachers who actually looked out for him, but not enough to change any situations.

So while they ignored him and we tried to help him, Dawson turned to the darker side of high school life. The jocks didn't like him, he wasn't a kid who played sports, and he was gay. So they didn't want him in the locker room. The smart kids didn't want him. He struggled in every class. The only club he was in was the student council. He seemed to like that, and we were encouraged. Dawson very quickly fell in with girls from broken homes who struggled with life and were already making poor choices. He found escape by being high. He was working at McDonald's as well. We thought that this was good. He would learn how to do a job, make some money and friends, and get some social skills. It turned out that some of the other employees there used drugs, and even a manager would join in, smoking pot with the employees late at night. He hid all this life from us, and we simply did not know.

Finally, he graduated from high school. He had good enough grades to get into Indiana Tech in Fort Wayne. You didn't need high grades to get in; you just needed money! Four-year private college. Two hours from home. We figured it was far enough away to feel independent, close enough to come home or for us to visit. We attended orientation. We were told that there was no way a student could fail out of Indiana Tech. The speaker listed several ways for students to get help and, over and over, the fact that they should get help the minute they felt they were falling behind.

We were optimistic. Dawson seemed excited. He was fooling us completely. His thoughts were that he could be away and be high all the time. He didn't care about school at all. He was going through the motions so he could do whatever he wanted. We went for a family day a couple of months into his freshman semester. He had barely rolled out of bed before we arrived. We had Rachel with us and Tony's parents and Great-Grandma Ethel. We were so excited to explore the school and see how he was doing. Twenty-twenty hindsight has shown me that he was high from the night before. Maybe hungover as well. We thought he was tired from classes and studying. Maybe we just didn't want to see the truth. He assured us he was getting As and Bs. One lie after another.

He seemed to have a few friends there that were good supports from what we could tell. Turns out one very good friend was a very good enabler. There was just one friend who truly cared about him. This particular friend texted me the following spring, telling me Dawson was failing everything, using drugs, drinking, and was in danger.

We were so proud of Dawson on that family day in October 2017. The sun was shining. There were food trucks and a band playing. The school seemed to be just the thing he needed. We were so proud.

Our son, who had been lost for so long, was finally a college student, and was doing so well—we thought. We traveled home that day, feeling good, happy that he was finally free of bullies and pain. What we didn't know was that he had already started skipping classes, had found the worst people he could in Fort Wayne, and was getting high every day. He had also been sneaking home on the weekends, staying with some of the girls here he had hung out with in high school.

He even changed his address to one of theirs, so when the letters saying he was failing were mailed, they didn't come to us. The lies he told and the life he was living was spiraling out of control, and we had no idea whatsoever. On my knees each night, I thanked God for

Dawson being in college, finding his way and doing well. I trusted that he was safe and happy. I could not have been more wrong.

Fall of 2017 merged into winter of 2018. Dawson wasn't home much. Rachel was really busy, leading clubs, farrowing pigs, getting ready for all things seniors do! She was applying for scholarships and visiting colleges. She settled on IUPUI. They have the only school of philanthropy in the world, and she was accepted there. Tony and I were anticipating an empty nest, with two kids successfully in college, and we could get back to, well, whatever it is people do *before* they have kids! I'd wander into Dawson's room sometimes and look at the things he'd left behind. My heart would swell with missing him and with pride, thinking he was doing well in college and finding himself and discovering life.

I was happy and sad with missing him at the same time. Rachel kept me busy with her events and getting ready for graduation. It was a transitional time. Tony was getting ready for spring planting. I was busy working for the CASA program. With CASA, you advocate for kids whose parents either neglect or abuse them. DCS has entered their lives, along with attorneys and court hearings and strangers. CASAs are the constant person in the kid's lives and you advocate for them in court. You're the only person who stays with them from the beginning to the end of their case.

I felt I did my job very well. I thought I knew kids pretty well. I had families tell my boss about how much their kids liked me. Again, little did I know that my kid was lying to my face and had an entirely secret life I knew nothing about. So when it all came to light, not only did I feel like the worst mother in the world, but I also felt that I couldn't *possibly* be a good CASA. How could I help other peoples' kids when mine was so broken and I had no idea!

I received an anonymous text on March 22, 2018. I was actually just getting out of my car to visit some of my CASA kids. I looked at the unknown number's text and read, "Hi, Patti. I used to go to college with your son, Dawson. I feel like you should know that he is on a bad path to self-destruction. Last semester, he failed all his classes. He is doing drugs, hence the fact that he doesn't have any money. My friends and I have told him to slow down and catch up on schoolwork, but he continues on the same path. He did have one friend who tried to help keep him in line, but I don't know how well that went. I just feel like you care about him a lot. He is wasting your money, and I think you need to speak to him. I wanted to tell you before, but I was afraid."

I remember my knees buckling. My heart was pounding, and it was hard to breathe. I got right back in my car and called Indiana Tech. I finally got someone on the phone. They said they could only tell me whether or not he had been going to class. They put me on hold for what seemed like forever. They finally came back and said he hadn't been to class in three months since the start of the semester. They then said he was failing out of school and we needed to do something about it. I demanded to know why we were just then being told and only because I had called. They said they'd sent a letter in fall, stating he was failing. Of course, we had never received that, because he'd changed his address to one of the girls here and it went to her house. Her dad never said a word to us about our son's mail going to his house.

I asked the man on the phone what to do, and he said we could come get him anytime. But it was too far into the semester for us to get any money back whatsoever. Of course. What did I expect? I hung up and called Tony in a frantic state of tears and yelling. He wasn't sure what I was saying at first. I finally got the words out and headed home. He met me there and read the text. We got in my car and started driving to Fort Wayne. I contacted a school counselor to let them know what was happening. At that point, I didn't know what kind of drugs he was using. I didn't know if he'd become violent or if he was passed out in his room or worse. I didn't know if he'd try to run from us, come at us violently, or what. The woman said she would meet us in the cafeteria and we'd walk over to his dorm.

It was so surreal. That day, I had received an email from the New York Institute of Art and Design. I'd taken the time to finally get a diploma of a sort, and that very day, I received word that I had passed with a certificate in personal style. I was so excited, and then the bottom dropped out of my world. Quickly before we left for Fort Wayne, we made the decision to stop at the high school and pull Rachel out of class to tell her what was going on. We didn't know what kind of nightmare we were going to be walking into, and we wanted to let her know it might be quite some time before we returned home that day. She was very upset, and we were all in tears as we told her what was going on.

Two hours later, we arrived at Indiana Tech. We got to the cafeteria, and the school counselor was there waiting for us. She confirmed that he had flunked out and we needed to return the schoolbooks. And again, we wouldn't be getting any kind of refund. We were talking about all this when I looked up and saw Dawson walk into the cafeteria. He was looking down at his phone. He looked gaunt and disheveled, thin under a leather jacket. His hair was longish and messy. He was walking and looking down at his phone, but then he looked up. He stopped in his tracks, staring at us.

Then he came to me quickly and hugged me hard. He started to cry and apologize. He said over and over he was going to call us that very day. I didn't believe him at all. I think he would have just stayed in Fort Wayne with the people he was doing drugs with and couch-surf until he ended up on the streets. Tony hugged him too, and the lady said for us to go to his dorm room and clean it out. So we walked that way, saying nothing. The pale sun of spring shone as we crossed the street to the dorm. Birds were chirping. People were going to classes, smiling and oblivious to the nightmare we were slogging through.

We got to his room. His bed and desk area were a mess. The sheets were unwashed for who knew how long. Dust covered every surface. Trash overflowed the wastebasket and was all over the floor. His roommate's side of the room was very neat and tidy. I was sickened by Dawson's chaos. I was angry and started stuffing things into bags and picking up trash. I remember cleaning the bathroom for the sake of the roommate. Dawson wanted to talk to Tony alone in the hallway. I just kept cleaning, going from tears streaming down my face to incredible anger to the point that I literally saw red. My ears were ringing, and my heart was pounding. I was beyond hurt and was furious at him for what he had done—using and manipulating us, spouting off endless lies about everything in his life. He and Tony came back in. By then, I was almost throwing things. I couldn't even speak. I bagged up all the textbooks and left a note for the roommate, asking him to please return the books. I'm sure he was incredibly relieved to get rid of Dawson.

A friend of Dawson's showed up in the midst of this. We took her and Dawson to get something to eat so he could say goodbye to her. She had a list of excuses as to why he was failing and claimed to be trying to help him. Of course, later, he admitted to giving her his paraphilia to hide from us. She was going to mail it to the girl at home whom he had changed his address to keep for him. This girl in Fort Wayne was also going to send him some kind of drug that would mask the pot in his system so he could pass the drug tests. What a great friend, right?

The next day, we took him to our pediatrician. At nineteen, he had passed the age cap to be seen by her, but she loved Dawson and cared about our family and wanted to see him right away. She still sees him, in fact. She is a true treasure. She recommended a counselor down in Kokomo. We took him there a couple of times. He told us he didn't like her. I got him set up with another one in Rochester, half an hour from home. He spent months lying to her and getting high on his way home after his appointments. He got pulled over one day, and they found pot in his car. He wasn't arrested but only because the jail there was full. He didn't tell us about this. We only found out when mail started coming home from defense lawyers. I finally opened one up, and it stated that he had a pending case! Once again, we were shocked. Immediately we confronted him, and he told us what had happened. We went to court, and he was appointed to a public defender, whom he was to meet with at a later date. My sweet, loving little boy, who picked me dandelions, was becoming this dark, lying, manipulating addict who might now be headed for jail!

We kept him at home so that no one would ask why he was out of school at the end of March. We tried to get him to just relax and heal, focus on getting better. Finally, we let him go back to work at McDonald's. He'd been begging to for weeks. We still didn't know he was smoking dope with one of the managers there. It makes me beyond sick to think a manager would do this with a young employee. What else does this woman do with young kids? Where are her morals?

Rachel was angry and scared. She retreated into her activities and stayed busy all the time. She didn't want to talk about any of it much. She became distant and shut down when we tried to talk to her. My heart broke further. How could he hurt himself and all of us so much? Couldn't he see what he was doing to the family? Obviously, he did not. One night, I came home from my part-time job in Logansport at Cato. It was about 10:00 p.m. Dawson was sitting on a barstool in the kitchen. Tony and Rachel were standing by him. I asked what was going on. Dawson was crying. Tony told me to go upstairs with Rachel. I followed her to his room. Thirteen trash bags were stuffed with all his clothes were sitting on the floor. The TV was gone. The Xbox I'd bought him for his birthday just a few months before was gone. We went back downstairs. Tony said Dawson sold the TV and Xbox on Let Go. Strangers came to my driveway, and he sold those things to them.

I just stared at him. I asked why. Well, he was going to call a taxi and go back to Fort Wayne to live with that great girl (friend) and her grandma. He wanted away from us and our rules. He wanted out. I just stared at him. We had just bailed him out of school and brought him home. We didn't kick him out for wasting our money on private college that he threw away for drugs. We hid him here so he wouldn't have to explain to anyone why he was home from college so early. We had gotten him to the doctor and counselors. And this was the thanks we got. None of my friends knew what was going on. No one knew he was home. We were all keeping secrets for him, trying to help, aThis felt likslapped us in the face. Hard. This was so disrespectful and disgusting.

I just looked at him. I had crossed my arms over my chest, completely frozen. Dawson was crying and said he felt like he'd just lost me as his mom. I didn't respond. In that moment, I was totally done with him. I felt rage snake through my heart. How *could* he do this to us? And once again thought, *I must be the* worst *mother in the world. Look how my son wants to run away from love and support.* I could barely breathe. It was so incredibly painful. We convinced him to stay and pushed through another month of unease and anxiety. I didn't realize at the time of course, that his actions really didn't' have anything to do with us personally. It was his need to escape from himself, no matter the cost. He wasn't trying to hurt us intentionally. It was the way he'd learned to cope with his life.

Soon it was May. Rachel was graduating. I remember looking at Dawson and saying, "Go ahead. Don't come to Rachel's graduation and see how that goes over." I was so angry with him all the time, I'd say hurtful things out of my own fears. I have a lot of regret for those conversations. He came. It was bittersweet. Here my son should have been finishing his first year of college, but he'd flunked out. Rachel would be a college freshman in the fall. She graduated third in her class. She won over $38,000 in scholarships! She was headed toward a very bright future. And there was Dawson, lost and not caring, not wanting to be well. He wanted drugs and, later we found out, alcohol. And other drugs too.

I couldn't even look at all the pictures I had of him around the house anymore. He had been a beautiful child, and now he had turned into this dirty, lying, stealing jerk. Where did we go wrong? Love, support, help college, a car. Where did we drop the ball for him to do this and hate us? Did we spoil him with too much? Probably. I couldn't understand at the time that it really wasn't us he hated; he didn't like himself. He couldn't find self-love and acceptance, so he was trying everything he could to escape from his truth.

Fair was coming up at the end of June. We'd been on pins and needles with Dawson. We couldn't trust him at all. He wouldn't always show up to work at McDonald's and wouldn't be where he would say he would be when he went out with friends. This was Rachel's tenth and final year with 4H. She would be showing pigs, competing in public speaking, in the running for 4H royalty and also the county queen pageant. We were all busy helping her get ready for all this and keeping an eye on Dawson at the same time.

I came home again from my job at Cato on Sunday afternoon, the day before the fair would start. Tony's dad and stepmom were here, along with his dad's sister. They'd been out and about and had stopped by. I pulled in and got out of my car. Tony came out of the porch, crying. Everyone was looking down. My heart dropped. What had happened now? We'd already had instances of Dawson not showing up to work and McDonald's calling, looking for him. He'd lied so many times about where he was and whom he was with. We'd taken his phone and the car away. He was basically grounded. I'd gone through his phone several times. He'd written to people about how he hated us so much, that we were psychopaths and stupid. He hated our house rules and wanted to be free to come and go as he pleased, use drugs, drink, and hang out with all his friends that did that too. He bragged about what a good liar and manipulator he'd become, telling us lies and sneaking around. It made me sick when I'd read his phone.

The pictures of him getting high were crushing. How could this be happening? I had no idea what Tony was going to say through his tears. "He's gone. He's gone." Over and over, that was all he could say. I didn't know what he meant! Did he mean gone as in dead? Or gone as in left? Finally, he choked out the words that Dawson had run away. He'd snuck out of the house and taken off on foot when Tony was mowing the pasture. Tony had called the police. They came here and told him that because Dawson was nineteen, there was nothing they could do for at least a month! Tony went looking for him at McDonald's. They called the police, and Tony was banned from

McDonald's for life! He went there, looking for Dawson. He raised his voice to the people working there, who were hiding Dawson in the back room. It was horrible. We asked the police if they would at least do a welfare check, if they could find him at McDonald's. They did and said he was there, but they couldn't make him come home. In the eyes of the law, he was an adult.

So the fair started. Rachel again won public speaking. Then she won 4H Royalty!

Dawson wasn't there. It was so bitter yet so wonderful for her at the same time. I didn't know how to feel. We didn't know where Dawson was. Was he alive? Was he sleeping on the ground somewhere? Was he with bad people? Was he safe? How could we sleep? How could we function? How do we cheer for Rachel while our minds were wild with worry for Dawson? The next day was it. The pageant—it was exciting and thrilling and happy all at once. The pageant started. . My friend Tara was sitting with me.

Tony wandered the edges of the stage area, watching Rachel and looking around for Dawson at the same time. He wasn't there. Rachel was crowned Miss Pulaski County 2018,

and her big brother wasn't there. He was off somewhere, probably getting high. It was her moment, and he caused so much pain by not being there. I was beyond thrilled for Rachel. She had just won public speaking, 4H Royalty and now queen of the county! It doesn't get better than that! Only two other girls had ever won 4H royalty and then queen the next day in the history of our town. I was bursting with pride for my girl. And then my heart was shattering, and my soul was dying because my son was missing. Was he alive? We didn't have any way to know.

The next evening was the talent show. The boy Dawson was seeing was in the talent show and what do you know, there was Dawson. I was talking to a friend around the corner from the stage, while Tony walked to the talent show area. He quickly motioned for me to come to him. He pointed to across the arena, and there was Dawson, talking to some people. He was skinny and looked dirty. We quietly approached him. He saw us, but he didn't come to us. He looked like he wanted to run. But of course, he was there to see his boyfriend, so he didn't. We sat by him to talk. He had bruises on his neck. It looked very much like fingerprints on one side and a thumbprint on the other, as if he had been choked. Rachel, in her crown and sash, was seated on the opposite side of the arena, watching the talent show. She glanced our way a few times but made no move to come over. She was in the spotlight now as the new queen, and she was not going to draw attention to Dawson with his obvious drug use.

I couldn't stop tears from running down my face as I spoke to Dawson. He was visibly impaired. Glassy-eyed and not able to focus on us. We told him we were so happy he was at least not dead. He refused to say where he was staying. He refused to come home. He said he was still working at McDonald's. He said what we thought were bruises were just hickeys from his boyfriend all over his neck. We didn't believe him. We finally left the arena and let him be. We did get him to promise he would stay in touch with us so we would at least know he was alive. It was a very real concern.

The fair continued through the week. Rachel showed her pigs and did well. She handed out ribbons and trophies. Auction night came, the final fair for her. She had tears as she walked her pig to the arena. She smiled through her tears as the long ten years of 4H and all her accomplishments faded into her past. Her crown glittered and sparkled. She was so beautiful. My heart ached with a mother's love and pride as I watched her sell a pig for the last time. Her queen's kiss was auctioned, and Tony paid over $3,000 for it. She was all over the front page of the paper and throughout from fair week. I saved them all for her and made her a scrapbook. This marked time in her life was overshadowed by Dawson's choices and decisions. He had rocked our family to its core, and we were in survival mode. We weren't able to enjoy Rachel's final fair like we should have been able to.

Rachel spent her summer going to other county pageants. She was in several parades, had speaking engagements, and spoke at another pageant as well. She was also getting ready to go to college, and I took her to orientation for a couple of days at IUPUI.

Dawson finally relented and said he would live with Tony's grandma Ethel after he walked off the job at McDonald's. Or maybe he was fired. We didn't really know the truth. Ethel was ninety-two at the time. She loved Dawson very much. We decided that would be good. At least we'd know where he was. Tony helped Dawson get a job at a gas station near Grandma's house. He was probably twelve miles or so away from our house. Sometimes, if he were working late at the gas station, I'd stop on my way home from my job at Cato in Logansport. He'd be outside, smoking a cigarette. He always had hugs for me. Watching him smoke made me sick. I used to smoke years ago, so I tried not to say anything to him about it. At least he had a job, I thought. At least he was safe at Grandma's. Of course, later we found out he was getting high in his room upstairs at her house. He was also sneaking out almost every night to go see his boyfriend some fifteen miles away, then getting high or drunk or both and driving back to Grandma's at four in the morning. No wonder he'd sleep till two or three in the afternoon. Again, we had no idea.

The summer wore on. Dawson got fired. They said he stole some food at the end of the day. He said he'd forgotten to pay for it and was going to pay the next day. Then he said the manager hated him because he was gay and that was why he got fired. Being gay was his excuse for that, his excuse for using drugs and drinking too, pretty much anything he didn't want to take responsibility for. It was all because he was gay and got bullied all the time. It was never his fault. Eventually, he got a job as a host at Applebees in Logansport, where I had my part-time job at Cato. He'd walk across the parking lot on his smoke break to come see me sometimes. He was wearing foundation and other makeup by that time, trying to hide hickeys on his neck, trying to hide his face from the world. His boyfriend was big into full makeup and looked more like a drag queen than anything else most of the time. Dawson was convinced he was so ugly he had better wear makeup to show that he was handsome. Dawson had always been very good-looking—perfect eyebrows, brilliant blue eyes, square jaw, full lips. He was really handsome, but he didn't believe it at all.

Applebees fired him. He wasn't showings up for his shifts. Or if he did, he was late or high or usually both. By then, it was fall. Rachel had gone on to win grand champion public speaking at the Indiana State Fair! We were so proud of her. Dawson wasn't there for that either. Her anger toward him continued to grow. Her distance from us increased. I was glad she was in college and had other things to focus on besides the mess that our family was turning into. My heart hurt with the growing distance between her and us. But I knew she had to find her own way to cope. Summer had ended. The dandelions wilted and died.

It was nearing Halloween. Every year, we would get a campsite at the state park, just north of town. It was a tradition with Tony's sister and her family and us. They have a *huge* Halloween weekend out there with decorations and hundreds of people. Rachel came home to hand out candy there as the queen. We were having a great time. We expected Dawson. He said he would come. He didn't. It was another letdown.

Next was Thanksgiving. He was there at Grandma's, of course. We all went there to eat. He was kind of distant. Most likely, he was high. We didn't know of all his drug use at that time, but it's probably a pretty sure bet that he was high.

Christmas was coming. Tony was done with harvest. Rachel was finishing her first semester as a freshman. Things were just okay. We didn't see Dawson much. Grandma would report that he was home every night. He told her he was job hunting. No, he wasn't. He was just waiting out the days till Grandma fell asleep, and out the door, he would go. I was working and had finished a second online certificate. Then came Christmas Eve. Rachel was home on break, and her boyfriend was with us for dinner. We were just waiting for Dawson. He finally showed up. High as a kite. His eyes were as shiny as Justin Bieber's in his mug shot that was all over the internet! Dawson was talking a mile a minute and being overly polite, kind of like how people were when they knew they'd had too much to drink but they wanted you to think they were totally sober.

I was heartbroken. Christmas Eve, and you come to my home high. He only came to get the Christmas card with money in it. He left pretty quickly after that. I was completely distraught. My sweet Dawson, totally unraveled. Using drugs, unemployed, failed out of college. What should I do now? How could I help him? How could I keep my own act together? It was all I could do to get through a day and do my job and believe that my son was going to be okay somehow, some way. I cried myself to sleep every single night.

Three days later, on December 28, Dawson turned twenty. He had some of his girlfriends over to Grandma's house. Upstairs they drank and got high. I have seen photos on his phone showing this. He wouldn't come to our house for his birthday or go out to dinner. He said he'd come over the next day to get his birthday card, but he'd be too busy to stay long, of course. He had drugs to buy with that birthday money. We found out later, too, that he was stealing from Walmart and other places to sell things and buy drugs or steal things to give to his boyfriend as presents so he would like Dawson more.

That next day, I had gone to Walmart in Logansport, and on my way home, I called Dawson to ask when he was coming over. He said he had to shower and then he'd be there. He said he couldn't stay long. He gave me some excuse as to why. I felt tears prick my eyes, as I knew wherever he said he had to be next was a total lie. He just wanted the money and to go get high with his friends. Photos all over his phone showed him with mounds of pot and pipes and lighters and all his friends laughing it up, drinking, and smoking. Tears I had shed seemed to know no end with all I had seen.

I got home and put away my groceries and lit candles around the house as I always did. I worked on some laundry and glanced at the clock. He still hadn't shown up. Where was he? He should have arrived at least ten minutes ago. I started to pace around, debating whether to call him. The hairs on the back of my neck stood up. I shivered. Something was wrong. I felt it. Knew it. I put on my boots and paused again to look out the kitchen window. Suddenly, all my lights went dim. My heart began to pound. Something was very wrong. I felt it with every fiber of my being. I grabbed my phone and dialed his number. No answer. I grabbed my coat. Sirens started to blare. I looked out the kitchen window again. Far off, south on the highway through the trees, I saw police lights. I knew. It *had* to be Dawson. More sirens, probably ambulance. I dialed his number again as I struggled into my coat. A woman, a stranger, answered the phone.

"WHERE'S DAWSON!" I screamed into my phone.

"Honey, I don't know. There's been an accident. I pulled over. I heard a phone ring. I found it lying in the field, so I answered."

I screamed, "Is HE ALIVE?"

"Honey, I don't know. I'm sorry! I'm going to give this phone to the officer."

I jumped in my car and sped out to the highway. I kept dialing Tony's number. He didn't answer. I knew he was just across the highway in the hog barn. There was no reception in there. I kept dialing and dialing. Within minutes, I was at the crash site. The Saturn SUV was sitting in a cornfield. The entire roof was flattened. It was level with the hood of the car. There was an electrical pole that had been snapped completely in two. I jumped out of my car and ran toward the demolished dark-gray Saturn. Cops started running toward me, yelling at me to get back and warning me of live wires down.

(These are photos of the SUV after it was towed from the accident scene.)

I stopped and yelled, "THAT'S MY SON! THAT'S MY SON! IS HE ALIVE?"

No one would answer me. I was jumping up and down and screaming over and over, demanding to know if he was alive. They had that blue tarp lying on the ground next to the car. The one they draped over dead bodies at accident scenes. It was completely surreal. I felt as if I were in a movie. This couldn't really be happening.

I'd hear about accidents and see them on the news almost every day, but I thought it wouldn't happen to my family.

No, it can't be happening right now.

They finally said, "He has a pulse. Now get back in your car, and let us do our job!"

I somehow climbed back into my car and finally was able to reach Tony. Again, I was screaming! "GET IN YOUR TRUCK AND HEAD SOUTH ON 35! DAWSON'S BEEN IN A WRECK! HE MIGHT DIE! GET HERE NOW!"

I don't think Tony understood me at first, and I kept yelling and yelling about what was happening. He finally seemed to understand, and I could almost hear the diesel as he cranked it up and sped toward the scene. As soon as I saw the white Dodge, I jumped out of my car again. He ran toward me, and we together ran toward the Saturn. They had used the Jaws of Life to get Dawson out of the car and were loading him into the ambulance. I tried to climb in with him, but they wouldn't let me. They just said to meet them at the Winamac hospital. We found out later that he had been so close to death and they didn't think he would live to make it to the hospital so they didn't let me in the ambulance.

I got back in my car and told Tony to meet me just up the highway at our house. We got there, and I was gathering my thoughts, trying to make sense of this nightmare we had suddenly been thrown into. I went into the house and blew out the candles. I called Rachel for the third time. When I couldn't reach Tony at first, I'd called her. She and her boyfriend, Kyle, were headed toward the accident. I told them to just go straight to the hospital. I called Tony's sister then and broke the news to her. We wanted her to go to Grandma Ethel's house and tell her so that she wouldn't find out some other way. The news in small towns travels like wildfire By then three or four people had already called me! Terri graciously headed there, while we got in my car and headed to the hospital.

We got there just after the ambulance did. They had him in an emergency room. They wouldn't tell us much. We made more phone calls. Rachel and Kyle got there. It was a blur of tears and hugs. They wouldn't let us see him and wouldn't say why. After nearly an hour, the doors opened, and people pushing a gurney took someone down a short hall to another room. It was Dawson, and I didn't even recognize him! He was so bloated. I truly didn't know it was my son! They had taken him for a CT scan to send to South Bend Memorial Hospital. They finally told us they were waiting for a special ambulance team from another town to make the drive. They couldn't go by helicopter. The weather had turned worse—sleet, freezing rain. They were not optimistic. They finally brought him back from the CT scan and allowed us into the room.

He was strapped to a gurney because his arms and legs were flailing about. There was a nurse squeezing a rubber oxygen bag that covered his nose and mouth, breathing air into his lungs.

I looked at her and said, "He can't breathe on his own, can he?" More of a statement than a question.

She looked at me and shook her head, "No, this is breathing for him."

His eyes were closed. His shirt had been cut off him. There were electrodes on his chest. His arms and legs were jerking in every direction. There were several nurses and an ER doctor. The EMTS that brought him in were still there. There were a couple of cops too. I looked at each person in the room. Not one person would meet my eyes. They looked everywhere but at us. It was eerily quiet, monitors beeping. I could hear phones ringing. I leaned over and spoke to

Dawson's closed eyes. We all took turns telling him we were there and loved him. I didn't know if he could hear us. The impact of the crash had knocked him into a coma.

After what seemed like hours, the other EMT team showed up. They were all giving directions to the hospital team, and they got him on their gurney to go. Someone took over bagging him so he could get air into his lungs. We each kissed him before they loaded him into their ambulance. They told us they would go right down 14 East and hit 31 North and we shouldn't try to keep up. We sent Rachel and Kyle back to the house to pack clothes for us. Then we started down the highway, following the ambulance. The slick roads kept them at about 60 miles per hour. Tony and I were in a state of shock, following the ambulance that held our son, who was fighting for his life.

Tony's phone rang. It was the neurosurgeon from South Bend Memorial. He said he didn't know if Dawson would survive the ambulance ride, but if he did, the OR team was waiting and he was going to remove the left side of Dawson's skull. He said there was major swelling from the images that the Winamac hospital had sent to him. He would be draining blood and fluid off Dawson's brain. He was not convinced Dawson would survive the ride there. I was on my phone, contacting people. I don't even remember whom I called. Probably my boss and some close friends. My parents and only sibling had passed away, so I had no family to call. I felt very much alone and terrified.

The ambulance reached highway 31 North, and we quickly lost sight of it. We turned to each other and had to have the conversation about organ donation. It was a very real possibility that that was what we would be facing in a few hours. The sky darkened as we drove. We finally got to the hospital but weren't sure where to park. We found a parking garage, and as we were walking towards the door, the ambulance team came out. They said he had survived the ride and was in surgery. We thanked them for all their help and entered the hospital.

After figuring out we were at the totally opposite end of where we needed to be, we spent another twenty minutes walking to the surgical waiting room. It was evening by then. Maybe 7:00 p.m. No one was around. Most of the lights were off. It was quiet, eerie in a way that hospitals were at night. Rachel had been able to reach Dawson's boyfriend through social media. He and his mom were on their way there. Rachel and Kyle got there, and we waited and stared at the clock and waited some more.

Finally, the surgeon stepped through a door. He said Dawson was alive. He was in a coma from the accident. He had a lot of brain swelling, so they had removed the whole left half of his skull. Dr. Shaikah went on to say that there was bruising all through his brain. He said he put draining tubes under his skull to drain blood and fluid. He then told us he didn't know if Dawson would wake up the next day or week or month or ever. Brain injuries were mysteries; they just didn't know. He said youth was on Dawson's side. He'd just turned twenty the day before, after all. He seemed optimistic from that point, but he truly didn't know what would happen.

Dawson had been taken to ICU, and we were going to be allowed to see him. We made our way to the ICU doors, and they let us in. Tony and I stood there. I think Rachel was with us as well. I can't quite recall anymore. It was quiet and fairly dark since it was nighttime and they kept the lights low. His head was bandaged up all the way around. There was dried blood on his face, as well as bruises. He had a cut on his wrist. The crazy thing was, he didn't break one bone in his body or any other big injuries. But I'd have traded broken bones for this horrible brain injury. Tony was crying, and we were stroking Dawson's hands and kissing his cheeks.

The nurse was there. His name was Phil. He told us exactly what drugs they were giving him and what was going on. He reassured us that he was safe and being monitored constantly. The ventilator tubes were in his mouth, down into his lungs, breathing for him. We watched the monitor and listened to the sound of the machine keeping our boy alive.

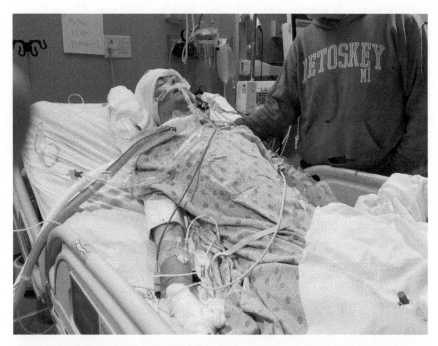

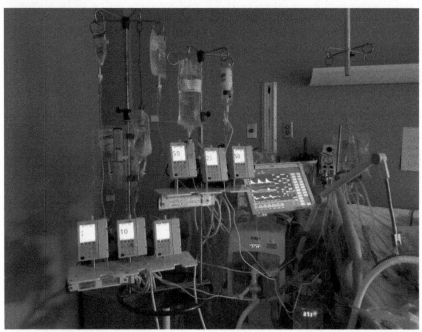

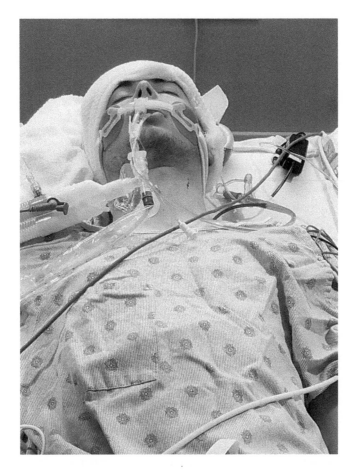

After a bit, it was time to go. Dawson's boyfriend and his mom left and headed home. The nurse directed us to a pastor that was there for families. He was from the Islands and so had that wonderful accent. He prayed with us and then gave us a list of nearby hotels. We went to one just across the street. The restaurant bar in it was still open, and none of us had eaten. We weren't really hungry but knew we needed to eat. We had to be alert and together for Dawson.

CHAPTER 2

So Tony, Kyle, Rachel, and I got a booth and stared at menus. The bar was busy, as it was almost New Year's Eve. There was a big hockey classic game that would be played at Notre Dame on New Year's Day. Kyle and Rachel had planned to go to it. The people there in the bar were all having a great time and watching sports on the many TVs. The four of us sat shell-shocked, wondering what to do next. The waitress was friendly and asked if we were there to party. We explained why we were there, and then she felt bad for asking! I felt sorry for her; it was awkward. We went to our rooms after we ate and tried to make sense of it all.

At 3:00 a.m., the phone rang, jerking us out of restless sleep. It was the hospital, asking for our okay to put Dawson on fentanyl! Of all the scary drugs, that one was terrifying. I knew fentanyl was a deadly drug on the streets but decided that if they felt he needed it, they could use it. They knew what they were doing in ICU. Morning dawned cloudy and cold. We gathered up our stuff and went back to the hospital, back to ICU. We met with nurses, and the neurosurgeon came in. He thought Dawson looked pretty good. They had removed the bandages from his head. It was frightening to see. They had shaved part of his head, but not all of it, which added to the craziness of it all. He had a line of staples from the front center of his forehead that formed a half-circle to the back and around to the front of his ear. Dried blood caked here and there. There were two tubes coming out of the top of his head, draining blood and clear fluid into rubber bulbs. His eyes were closed, and we saw no movement of his eyes behind them. No changes as far as him waking up. All the IV poles were pumping all sorts of drugs into him. We talked to him and stroked his hands, kissed him and rubbed his arms.

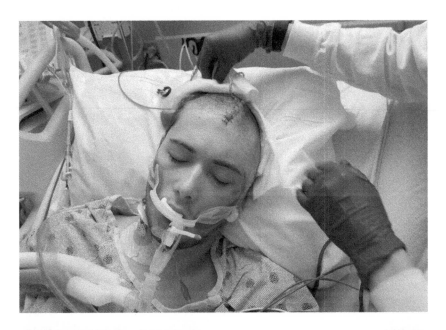

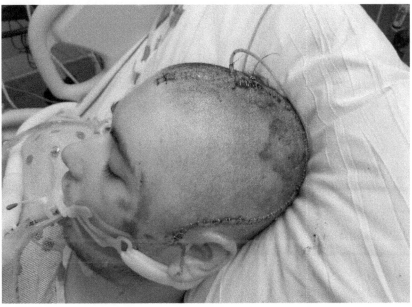

Tony's sister and Grandma Ethel came. It was heartbreaking to see her little ninety-three-year-old self reach over to Dawson's hand. She was devastated. We all took turns sitting with him or sitting in the waiting room. His boyfriend came up again with his mom. He went in a few times. Theirs was a rocky relationship, built on lies, cheating, drugs, alcohol, and bad friends all around. We were glad he was visiting Dawson, but we knew he wouldn't stick around. We had some conversations with him, and we explained that we didn't expect him to see it through. We didn't know when or even *if* Dawson would wake up. We didn't know if he would be a vegetable or would need round-the-clock care or what. His boyfriend was just eighteen and had plans to go away to college. We would certainly not expect him to care for Dawson. Who would or could at eighteen anyway? It wasn't fair to him or to Dawson. We didn't tell him he couldn't stay, just that we would understand if he didn't. Naturally, he came less and less, and in the end, he told Dawson that we pushed him out of Dawson's life. No way was he going to look like a bad guy. Dawson believed him and hated us. It was so untrue.

We went home during the day to wash clothes and repack. We were incredibly blessed to be able to stay in the Ronald McDonald House, which was attached to the hospital! We had always assumed only people who had babies in the NICU could stay at the house. Turned out that if your child was twenty-one or under, you could stay there. For free. We were there for sixty-six days. One night at the hotel was almost $300; sixty-six days in a hotel would have been financially devastating. The Ronald McDonald House was our saving grace all through January and February of 2019. The people there were incredible, and they stay in touch with us still. Tony and I would take turns, staying a stretch of days at a time. He would stay there while I went home to work, do laundry, regroup, and go back. Then I'd stay several days while he did things at the farm and took care of his pigs. They were all delivering their piglets right then, of course, so he had to be here for that.

Back in the ICU, Dawson did not wake up. The doctors said they needed to put the ventilator tube into his throat with a tracheostomy.

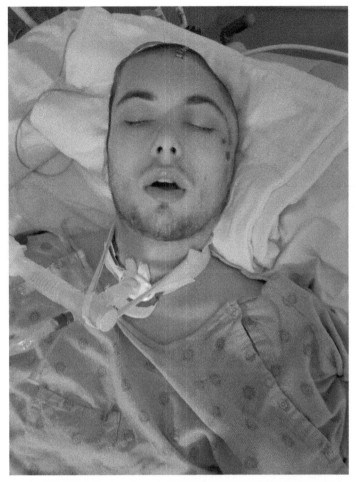

We had to sign papers for that. Then he couldn't eat, of course, so they had to put a feeding tube into his stomach. More papers. In the back of my mind, I could see dollar signs racking up, but when your child is lying there like that, unresponsive and hooked up to everything under the sun, you don't care what it costs. You just want him to wake up and be okay!

There was a window in Dawson's room in ICU, but there was a wall blocking any real view. The snowflakes piled up in the windowsill. Day by day, the snow climbed higher up the window as time passed. Or the bitter-cold wind would blow it all out of the window well, and then it would start to build up again. People say that cardinals are a sign of our loved ones from heaven coming to visit us. I noticed on the night of the accident, as Tony and I navigated the halls of the hospital, searching for the ICU unit, we passed the closed gift shop. In the window, I saw two wooden plaques with cardinals on them. I remember thinking, 'that has to be my parents, letting us know it will be ok.' I bought them both and put them on the windowsill of Dawson's room in the ICU. They brought me comfort.

We spent endless hours in his room, watching the monitors showing Dawson's heartbeat, listening to the ventilator breathe for him, watching the flickering lights of all six IV poles as they pumped so many drugs into his body, whispering words of love and support to him, kissing his cheek, holding his hand, rubbing his arms. I would give him baths with the wipes they had in the room. I cut his toenails. Tony and I both helped when he had to be cleaned up. They didn't have any kind of underwear on him, and so we cleaned him up count-less times with the patient care advocates. At first, they didn't want us to help, but that was our kid. We wanted to help. We felt helpless, so anything we could do, we did.

Tony's sister came several times and sat with Dawson for hours. She assisted the nurses as well with different things they were doing to help Dawson feel more comfortable, even though he was still in a deep coma. Dawson's boyfriend came a couple of times for a few hours. He didn't say too much. We tried engaging him in conversation about how Dawson had been doing previously. The boys had had a big fight recently, and we wondered if they had figured things out. We felt like Dawson's boyfriend was there more out of guilt than anything else. He told us many things, including how Dawson would steal things from Walmart and present them to him as gifts and that Dawson lied a lot, about almost everything, almost compulsively. He said Dawson drank sometimes but really liked getting high on pot. He confirmed that Dawson had tried pills as well.

As each admission was spoken, my heart broke a little more. I also became very angry at Dawson. How could he do all these terrible things? I was completely conflicted in my heart and mind. We had taught our kids that stealing was wrong, lying was never right, drugs were evil. We loved Dawson and had supported him through bullying and teachers that didn't take time to help him understand lessons. We helped him find a college he could go to and succeed at. The summer before his senior year in high school, we sent him to the computer camp at Indiana Tech. He said he had a great time and that it was what he wanted to do. He was focused and excited, he'd said. We believed him. He was lying. He was already into the drug culture, practicing ly-ing and manipulation. His texts on his phone spelled it all out for me in black and white. He hated us, told his friends we were psychopaths. He loved how he could lie and we would believe he was studying and doing well. It was a big joke to him. So as I gazed at his body lying there, the ventilator pushing oxygen in and out, keeping him alive, I was both heartbroken and furious at the same time. I had to leave the room for a while to try to sort out my feelings many times.

We were starting to fall into a routine by the end of the first week. We had brought enough clothes and toiletries and moved into a lovely room in the Ronald McDonald House. They truly saved our lives on many levels. It was wonderful. They provided hot meals each night, and snacks were available at any time of the day. You could even do your laundry there if you wanted to. The cafeteria had really good food, and we became somewhat familiar with the folks working there. Every person we encountered was friendly and helpful. I can't say enough good things about the people that work at South Bend Memorial Hospital. I'd go to the gift shop and buy things now and then. The ladies were pleasant and helpful every time. It started to feel like a family in a way.

When I would come home for a few days at a time, Sara, my boss and the CASA director graciously allowed me to come and go as I needed. I could participate in meetings by phone, instead of having to drive the two hours back from South Bend for them. She even filled in for me at court when I wasn't able to be there. I could not have asked for a better boss.

The people in ICU were respectful and caring above and beyond. Some of the PCAs (patient care advocates) would stop by Dawson's room to check in, even if they weren't assigned to him that day. One morning, I had the TV on quietly, and the movie *Mean Girls* was on. Dawson had always been a big Lindsay Lohan fan, and *Mean Girls* was one of his favorite movies, right behind *Freaky Friday*. Anyway, every time someone stepped into the room to check a line, take his temperature, check the IV fluids, or anything else, they would glance up and notice *Mean Girls* was on. Then they'd stay and watch a bit, and each one would comment on how much they liked that movie and how it was kind of a cult classic sort of a thing.

They started saying, "On Wednesdays, we wear pink." It was a line from the movie that Dawson lived by. Every Wednesday, he'd be wearing pink. So it was comforting and gave a little comic relief in the face of such pain. Dr. Shaikah would come by and check his head and the drains. He still could not tell us if Dawson would wake up or not. He didn't know. No one knew.

CHAPTER 3

January 4 came. It was the day of the Indiana State Fair Pageant. Rachel was competing along with eighty-seven other county queens from across the state. The pageant was held down at the state fairgrounds in Indianapolis. We'd been looking forward to it for months. Then all this happened. We had to go to support her, and we wanted to go. But here was Dawson, lying in a coma. We had extreme guilt because we wanted and needed to be there for Rachel. So I asked a dear friend of mine, Mashell, if she would come sit with Dawson so we could go to the pageant and feel okay about it. Mashell was a nurse. She was more than happy to come be with him for the two days we would be gone. We left on a bitter cold but sunny day and headed to Indianapolis. We had a room at a beautiful Victorian B&B. Once again, my close friend Tara came to the pageant and sat with me.

Each queen had to be interviewed by three judges. They asked her questions about her family and she revealed her brother was lying in a coma way up in South Bend because of an accident. The judges were shocked that she was even there but also impressed that she was holding it together so well. She didn't win the pageant, but she performed beautifully and gave a speech that brought us to tears when it was her turn on stage. The next day, she went back to school, as her winter break had ended. We headed back to South Bend. All in all, it was a nice break from the nightmare we were living. Our guilt slipped away, as we knew Dawson was in the safest place he could be and being cared for by supreme professionals. Mashell reported no changes several times to us while we were gone. We were so thankful for her caring friendship.

A few days after that, we had been to the cafeteria, taking a break, and when we got back to Dawson's room, there was his pediatrician, Dr. Eileen, standing there! I was stunned! We hugged each other tight and I said, "You're here, you're here! I can't believe you are here!"

She said, "Of course I am here. It's Dawson. It's the Ploss family! I came as soon as I heard!" She said that Dawson had youth on his side, just as the neurosurgeon had said. She was optimistic. She was positive and caring. She was *amazing*! She had to drive all the way to South Bend, to check on her patient who really was too old to be her patient, but she didn't care. She said she would see him until her bosses said she couldn't! Eighteen was the age limit for pediatricians' patients. He was twenty. She had seen him ever since then. She had seen us, counseling, advising, supporting. This incredible doctor, incredible person, is still supporting us through this journey.

We had received some mail from the court about an upcoming hearing Dawson had to attend regarding getting caught with marijuana in the car. The name and number of the public defender was enclosed. I called the lawyer, and his wife, who was also his secretary, answered the phone. She was in tears by the time I had explained it all. She said she'd have her husband call me. He called me the next day. He was very sorry about what had happened. He said there was not a lot of marijuana in the car. He said it wasn't a serious charge. He offered advice and prayer. We had a really interesting conversation. Again, a friendly person in the face of so much trauma. He said he would explain to the courts and the charges would be dropped. And he did, and they dropped it. While I was very thankful for that, I didn't want Dawson to someday think he could get out of trouble easily should it happen again.

Day 11 came. We were sitting there, as had become the norm for us. Suddenly, Dawson tried to sit up, and he turned his head toward me and opened his eyes!

This was the moment he opened his eyes. He looked right through me. His eyes were not focused, or even symmetrical.

I jumped up and leaned toward him. "Dawson! Do you see me? Can you hear me? It's Mom!"

He looked right through me. It seemed like he couldn't see me and was looking through my body and into the wall. It lasted just a few seconds, and he fell back and closed his eyes. We got the nurses in, and we all tried to gently wake him again. Nothing. I carefully pushed up his eyelid, but his eye was rolled back up in his head. But he had opened his eyes. Just for a fleeting moment. We were so excited and anxious for him to do it again.

The next day, it happened again, and he would have his eyes open for longer and longer moments. He didn't speak; he couldn't with the trach in his throat. His hands started to move around. He tried to grab the trach tube. He tried to reach the staples in his head. The nurses decided to tie giant white padded mittens onto his hands. The mittens were like boxing gloves; it had a net on one side so air could get to his fingers. They had laces as ties at the wrists. Well, Dawson was pretty smart under all the struggles he'd had. He would lift that mitten close to his face and study it. Then he would put it to his lips and bite and tug at those laces until he could untie that mitten and pull it off his hand with his teeth! We were astounded! Then he'd be pulling at the trach tube and everything else.

So then they had to tie his hands to the sides of the bed. And also his ankles. The feeding tube was at risk of being pulled out, the trach and IV lines too. They had to put a pic line into his upper left arm for all the IV needles to go in. He became more and more restless. He'd follow us with his eyes. He didn't try to talk. He just watched us. We'd ask him if he knew who we were. He'd shake his head no. It was crushing to us. I'd tell him I was his mom, and he would stare at me as if I were a stranger. I'd ask him if he knew what Mom meant. Again, no. Dawson became more alert, but he struggled to get his hands and legs free. Because they were concerned about him pulling the tubes out, they wouldn't untie him unless we were there to guide his hands away from tubes.

One day, he was very agitated and struggling to move. He managed to turn himself while tied down, hands and legs, over onto his belly! It pulled the trach tube right out of his throat! Nurses came running. Then doctors came too! They tried to reinsert the trach tube. Somehow, they got it down between his skin and breastbone and not into the space to his lungs, where it was needed to be. I was in the hall, looking into his room, as there were about ten people in there by then, all yelling and trying to fix it. On the loudspeaker, they paged any available surgeon to get to ICU *stat*! I was shaking and terrified. Tony was not there at the time. It was my day with Dawson.

What was happening? Dawson wasn't breathing, and they couldn't get the tube back into his lungs! I just stood there, waiting, watching, praying. Finally, they got it where it needed to be, and everything calmed down. I remember the doctor who had gotten the tube in the wrong place, trying to be casual about it to me, playing it off as not a big deal. I just stared at him and went back into Dawson's room to hold his hand and shed more tears. I didn't know I had more tears in me. I'd not cried so much for so long.

Another day, they decided they would turn off the ventilator to see if Dawson could breathe on his own. I was shocked they wanted to try this. They explained that they didn't want him to have the ventilator forever. He had contracted pneumonia by then, so they shut it off. Nothing. His chest stopped moving. He didn't breathe. The screen flatlined. My heart was in my throat by then!

In my head, I was screaming, *TURN IT BACK ON! TURN IT BACK ON!*

I asked how much longer before they'd turn it back on; he obviously wasn't breathing. After several seconds, they turned it back on. My heart slowed, and his chest started to move again. I was shaking from the experience of seeing my son not breathing. That was a long day.

A couple of days later, as Dawson was becoming a bit more alert for longer periods of time, the physical therapy team came in. They fitted Dawson with a soft foam helmet. They said they were going get him into a chair next to the bed. We were excited. As they helped him to sit up and swing his legs off the side of the bed, we watched with anxious curiosity. They got him into the chair and strapped him in so he wouldn't slide down onto the floor. They did this a few times a day for several days. One day, they came in and said they were going to stand him up!

What do they mean stand him up! I thought in my head.

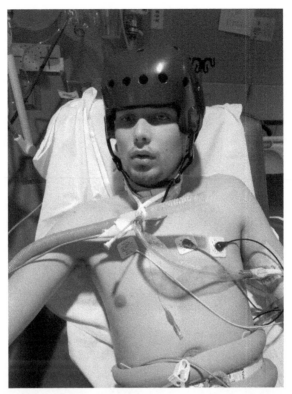

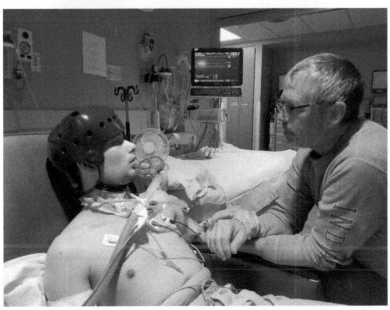

Tony was trying to tell Dawson who he was. Dawson was trying to talk, but couldn't. He didn't know who Tony was.

This kid was barely out of a coma and had been lying on his back for days. He was weak and barely conscious. But they were determined. There were three of them. They strapped on his helmet and secured a belt around his waist. Then they sat him up! His head fell forward. Drool fell from his lips as his head lolled back and forth. They spoke loudly to him about each thing they were doing as they did it. I stood back, astounded at their work. I saw him reach up with his hand to brush the drool away. They said that was more of a reaction than a thought process and deliberate. Then they stood him up! And he could stand! They held on to him with the belt, and the helmet was sliding down over his eyes.

He tried to take a step then the therapist said, "No, Dawson. You can't walk yet."

He turned and looked at her with the priceless look that seemed to say, "What do you mean I can't!"

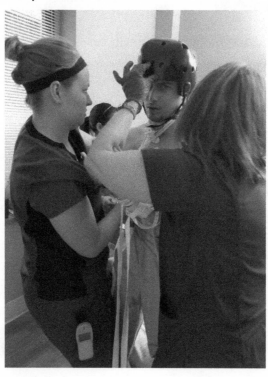

I snapped a picture of that moment, and it makes me grin when I look at it. They did this a few times a day for several days. The PCAs would come in many times a day and get him up and sit him down into the recliner chair. They always had to strap him in, because he would slide right down and almost on to the floor! Dawson still didn't know who we were or what Mom and Dad meant. Tony's sister Terri continued to visit, and Dawson's boyfriend showed up a few times. I could tell by looking at him that he was getting tired of it. The boy he used to be able to manipulate into buying weed and finding alcohol, the boy that would steal "presents" for him was not available now to do these things. Dawson didn't seem to really know who his boyfriend was, but he would look at him when he would visit.

Around that time, Dawson would grab the hand of anyone near him and kiss it. . It was endearing and made us all laugh. It could be a PCA, a nurse, a doctor, us, a therapist. Anyone he could reach out to and touch, they were getting kissed on the hand. Then he wanted to hug everyone. We took every ounce he was offering. Dawson had always been the best hugger! He could hug you so tight your back would crack. Of course, during the last year and a half, he would use those hugs to manipulate and try to make you think he actually cared about you when in reality, it was just another ruse to put something over on you and try to convince you that he was clean or doing things he was supposed to be doing, like working.

I took his hugs in the hospital because he was awake. Out of the coma. Getting better. I spent all those days, trying to let go of the horrible things he had put us through. He was so close to death for so long that any response from him now was a miracle. The staff started calling him their miracle man. Not one of them thought he would wake up. And if he did, they thought for sure he would be a vegetable. They all let him kiss their hands and hug them. They were so excited he was becoming more and more alert each day.

Dawson had become very thin, living on the protein shakes they pumped through the feeding tube in his stomach. I could see his hip bones poking out and his legs looking like sticks. I asked him if he was hungry, and he nodded his head yes. He still didn't speak. I asked about getting a swallow study for him. My boy was hungry, and I wanted to get food into him. He'd dropped twenty pounds in less than two weeks. They pushed back on the swallow study, and I pushed back harder to get it. So finally, orders were written, and someone came and did the study, so we were able to get them to feed him orally. On day 18, they said the next day, they would move him to the ninth floor, a step down from ICU.

That made us nervous. We wanted eyes on him at all times. They said they would continue having a sitter with him. They'd started that soon after he came out of the coma. A PCA would sit with him 24/7. They'd change out day and night shift. He was never alone. These people were saints! Sit in a room, watch someone lie in a bed, watch monitors, watch the person, just sit there—it was tiring beyond belief to do this as a parent, so for someone to watch a stranger they didn't know just lying there, it must be even more tiring. Of course, we would be there, too, a lot of the time, and we had great conversations with some of the sitters—some we didn't connect with at all, others we liked so much we requested them over and over again. So even though we didn't want to leave ICU, as we were so comfortable there by that point, we were reassured we'd have a sitter at all times.

By then, Dawson had developed MRSA and pneumonia. We had to wear a yellow gown each time we entered his room. MRSA is contagious. It stands for methicillin-resistant staphylococcus, which is a common thing for people who are in the hospital to get. The pneumonia was caused by the ventilator. It's a necessary evil of being on a vent. The vent pushes humid air into the lungs, the lungs become wet, and then you get pneumonia. But if the ventilator is removed too soon, you don't breathe, and then you die. A real catch 22.

We walked with the gurney to the elevator, and up we went to the ninth floor. It seemed very loud on the ninth floor. The dim quietness of the ICU was gone. There were people bustling about everywhere. Phones rang constantly, and people were paged over the loudspeaker every few minutes. It was scary and bright, and we worried about Dawson getting what he needed from nursing. In ICU, a nurse would only have two patients at a time. Up here on the ninth, they had maybe six or more. We got him settled in and met a nurse. She was all business and would not allow us to help change him or help him to sit him up or sponge-bathe him or anything. It was frustrating. We walked back to the Ronald McDonald House and looked out the window. We knew his room faced ours, as we'd looked out his window earlier. I couldn't determine exactly what room he was in, but I was going to figure it out one way or another.

A few days went by, and finally, they were going to allow Dawson to have some pureed food! This was a huge step forward! We got him sitting up in bed with his helmet on, moved the tray table up in front of him, and were ready when the tray of pureed food was brought in. We fed him with the silverware, and eventually, he would grab a spoon, much like a toddler. He couldn't get the food in fast enough. He was so hungry! We discovered he could suck out of a straw as well! They gave him as many milkshakes as he could drink! The pureed food and milkshakes were starting to put the weight back on.

He didn't always get the spoon or straw to his mouth, but he did his best. It was a lot like watching a toddler learn to feed himself. When I ask him now what he remembers of that time, he doesn't recall much at all. He will stare at me awhile and say he only remembers what I tell him happened. So they aren't real memories, just things people tell him. When Dawson looks at photos from the hospital, it's like looking at someone else he says. He has no memories, or feelings associated with physical pain or challenges.

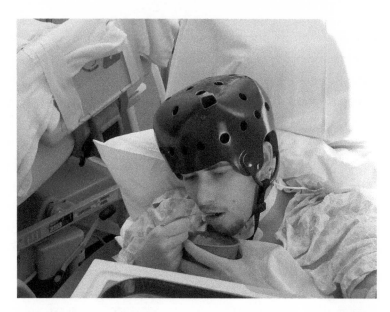

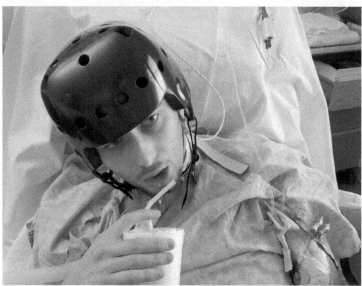

He still hadn't spoken yet, but he would watch us intently. Dawson was having a hard time seeing, as his glasses were destroyed in the wreck. So I called Walmart to see if they would replace them. They said his prescription was over a year old and he'd have to come in for a new exam. I explained the situation then, and they immediately relented on the rules and ordered him a new pair. Having new glasses on seemed to help him become more alert, because he could finally see more than a foot away!

The nurses on the ninth floor were hesitant to bring a chair into the room for us to get Dawson sitting in. They didn't think he was able to be moved. Again, I had to mamma-bear and insist they call PT, and they would tell them they had been working a lot with him. Finally, a chair was brought in. We would help move him to the chair, especially at mealtimes. Things were improving. We still had a 24/7 sitter, so that was comforting.

One day, Dawson was sitting in his bed, staring intently at his hospital wrist band. Suddenly, he spoke! He said, "Ploss, Dawson A. Twelve twenty-eight, ninety-eight." And he looked at me!

My mouth dropped open, and I exclaimed, "You can talk! You can read! Oh my god, Dawson!"

He nodded very seriously at me, and I asked him to read it again! And he did! I grabbed the hospital cafeteria menu and pointed to words. He could read and say them! I was crying by then, so excited, so happy, and so relieved! This was major! Tony couldn't believe it either!

After Dawson fell asleep for a nap, I went down to the gift shop to the toy section. They had one of those plastic screens with a met-al-tipped plastic pencil that you could use to write on the screen with. I bought it and a ball that lit up when you bounced it, a coloring book, and colored pencils. I grabbed a deck of UNO cards and regular cards as well. I took them back to his room and waited for him to wake up. I gave him the plastic screen with the pencil, and he wrote his first and last name on it and held it up! It looked like a preschool handwriting, but damn, he did it! He then drew more things on the plastic screen. He was engaged and alert. I gave him the coloring book and colored pencils and watched as he concentrated on coloring the pictures. I showed him the light-up bouncy ball. He watched the colors flash but was more interested in coloring and writing things.

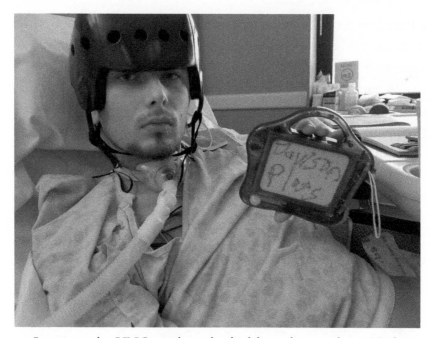

I got out the UNO cards and asked him the numbers. He knew some, not all. He knew the colors pretty well. It was exciting! I asked the sitter at the end of the day if she would bounce the ball in front of the window after I left and I would look for the flashing lights from my room at the Ronald McDonald House. She agreed, and I raced across the hospital and through the walkway over the street and down to my room. Sure enough, I could see the red flashing lights from his window way up high across the street. It was comforting to finally know which window was his. I would gaze up at it as I said my nightly prayers.

Dawson still wasn't sure about who we were. Or more exactly that we were his mom and dad. He still didn't seem to make that connection.

The next day, when I was with him, I asked him, "Dawson, who am I?"

His brows furrowed and seemed to think about who I was. Finally, he said, "You are Patricia Ploss," sounding out each syllable! No one calls me Patricia. Everyone calls me Patti.

I smiled at him and said, "Yes, that's my name, but you call me Mom. I am your mom. Do you know what that means?"

Again, his brows furrowed, and he slowly shook his head no and said, "You are Patricia Ploss." He knew Tony's name too. "Anthony Ploss." But he didn't understand the concept of mom and dad.

One day, Tony had been talking to Dawson and left while his sister Terri was there. Dawson said to Terri, "Who was that man?" Terri told him that was his dad. Dawson responded, "I'd like to talk with that man again soon." He just couldn't connect the dots.

Dawson asked repeatedly for Rachel. She would come every Friday from Indianapolis to see him. She sat by his bedside, and he played with her long blond hair. He didn't know who she was, even though she told him countless times. When she would leave, he would ask when Rachel was coming. We'd explain that Rachel had just been there, but he couldn't remember that she had just been there. He would insist that she had never come to see him. Then I would show him photos on my phone of her sitting with him and holding his hand. He would stare at the photos and say that wasn't Rachel. He didn't know who it was, but it wasn't his sister. His short-term memory loss was quite intense.

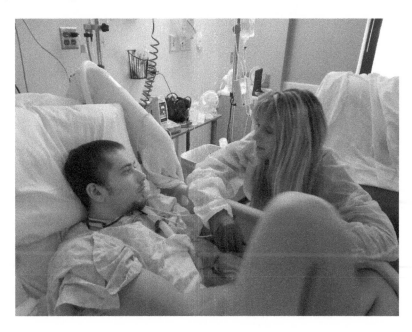

The days wore on. We got used to the loudness of the ninth floor. PT came frequently and got Dawson out of bed and walked him to his doorway and back to the bed. He wasn't allowed to walk down the hall because of the MRSA and pneumonia. The pic line team would come and clean and replace the pic line needles. This was especially hard for me to watch!

I'm no nurse! I would think, just as my mom would always say.

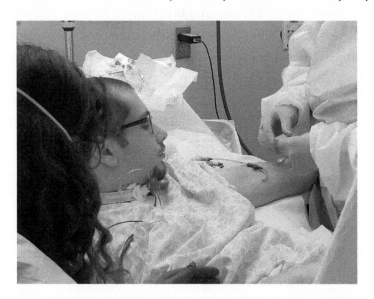

Dawson would watch them intently, but he didn't try to pull it out. The trach people would come and clean the trach apparatus and the hole in his neck. That, too, was not pleasant. I didn't watch too close. He would try all the time to grab the trach tuble and pull it out. They started downsizing the size of the trach tube so the hole in his neck would grow smaller. He was off tube feeding and eating pureed food. They left the peg in his belly, just in case they might need it again. Then we tried mechanical soft food, which is real food chopped up. He was able to handle that pretty well and was finally allowed to eat regular food! I would also order a tray from the kitchen, and we would eat dinner together every night that I was there.

Most of the time, Dawson had was is referred to as 'flat affect.' Meaning he would have a neutral expression on his face most of the time. I don't ever recall him smiling at all. He would stare intently at people, or things, but you could not tell what he was feeling or thinking. It took a few weeks for his eyes to level out once he woke up from the coma. His left eye wouldn't quite move in synch with his right eye. It was disconcerting to witness.

Then the neurosurgeon came. They were regularly doing CT scans, and they found that spinal fluid was pooling on the side of his head where he had no skull. Dr. Shaikah was concerned about this. He said it wasn't good for his brain and thought that if they put the skull piece back in, the fluid would find its way back down into his body and be absorbed.

The day came for that surgery. Dawson was to be taken to preop preparations at 2:00 p.m. They said we could sit with him while he waited for surgery. Then 2:00 p.m. came, and we followed the gurney down to the preop room. And we waited. And waited. And waited some more. At nearly 4:00 p.m., I was thoroughly angry. I went in search of a nurse. I was told that Dr. Shaikah was being held up with another surgery. In the meantime, Dawson had had nothing to eat or drink since the night before. I went back to the cubicle. He had to pee. You'd think I could find someone to get him a urinal, but no.. Then he couldn't hold it anymore and peed all over the bed.

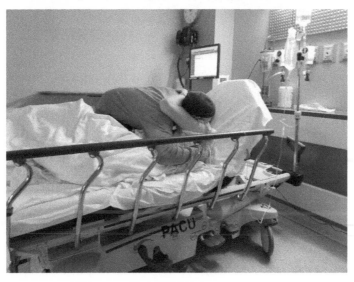

Tony and I cleaned him up and changed the bedding ourselves. Another hour or so went by. . They finally said Dr. Shaikah was still tied up and asked if we wanted to reschedule.

ARE YOU KIDDING ME! We've been waiting for hours. It's after 6:00 p.m. already!

We were going to wait. Dawson said he was okay. He'd drifted off to sleep several times. Another hour went by. For over six hours, we sat there in that preop cubicle. I was really upset because Dawson hadn't eaten in over twenty-four hours. He was thirsty, and they wouldn't do a thing. Finally, Dr. Shakiah and the anesthesiologist showed up and explained how they were going to replace his skull. Okay, fine, just get it done!

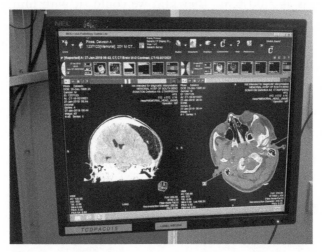

This scan shows the dark area of spinal fluid, pooling where there is no skull to protect his brain.

Tony and I waited again in the ICU waiting room. There weren't many people around. It was dark and quiet. It was after 11:00 p.m. when Dr. Shaikah appeared to tell us it went well and they'd drained all that spinal fluid. We went into ICU. We were in a different room this time, but we felt "at home," so to speak, back where it was quiet and there were eyes on the patient at all times. Dawson's head was wrapped in bandages again. The surgery had caused his left eye to swell nearly shut and blacken, as if he had been punched in the eye.

Just a side effect of brain surgery! He was barely awake. He kept reaching up to touch his head and feel the bandages. I don't think he knew what had been done to him.

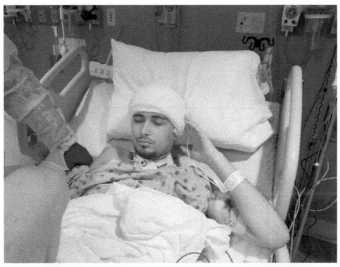

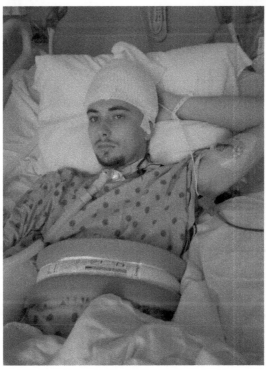

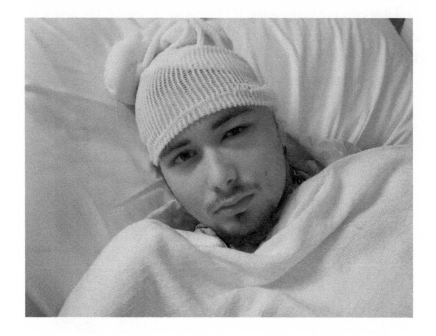

Around midnight, we were in the cafeteria, ordering Subway. They are open until 2:00 a.m. for people who needed to eat in the middle of the night. We were very thankful. Dawson spent just two days in ICU this time. The first time, he was there for eighteen days. Back to the ninth floor we went. Our very favorite PCA, Dan, visited us many, many times up on the ninth floor. He'd come on his breaks or after his shift ended. He even shaved the rest of Dawson's head and trimmed it all a few times once it all started growing back in. He was and continues to be a true friend. He said they didn't remember all the patients that came through ICU but that some stood out and they remembered those always. He said Dawson was one of those patients. Brittni, the nurse who had him the most in ICU and whom we just adored, would also come to see Dawson and check out his staples and pic line, trach and feeding tube. She wanted to keep an eye on her miracle man. We love these people so very much.

Another PCA, Jake, who often manned the door of ICU, was another favorite of ours. Jake was incredibly funny. When we learned his name one night, Tony looked at him and said, "Jake. Jake from State Farm? In khakis?" Like the commercial on TV. And this Jake was always in khakis. He laughed and said he got that a lot. It was almost irresistible to not say "Jake from State Farm" every time we greeted him. He'd often tag along with Brittni and Dan to come visit Dawson. It was so comforting when our team from ICU would come visit. They always offered assistance if we wanted or needed anything at all. Dawson continued to improve on the ninth floor. The trach tube was downsized every couple of weeks and finally removed. The pneumonia left, but the MRSA hung on. The yellow gowns we had to wear were becoming a wardrobe staple.

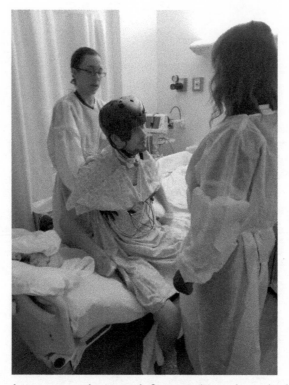

Speech therapy people visited frequently and worked with him on cognitive exercises, as well as talking, following a maze on an iPad, naming colors and numbers, learning patterns. He improved as the days passed. Aunt Terri continued to come when she could, she brought a memory game and played it with him often. Rachel would come on Fridays from Indy. It was so far to drive, but he would ask for her, and she would come.

Finally, they said they were going to move him yet again—this time, to the rehab unit on the fifth floor. He'd get physical therapy, speech therapy, and occupational therapy. We were again guarded and nervous about another move. He still couldn't walk and was slow to do things. They came one evening and removed the pic line from his arm. He watched them very closely. He wasn't talking too much at that point and sometimes said words that didn't go with the situation. His words would get scrambled, I guess you would say. He was so afraid it would hurt when they removed the line, that we had to hold his other hand back so he wouldn't grab it. When they removed the drains from his head, that hurt him, and he became wary of anyone who wanted to check staples or tubes. Removing the staples from his head took a little bit and was uncomfortable, and we had to hold him down for a lot of that.

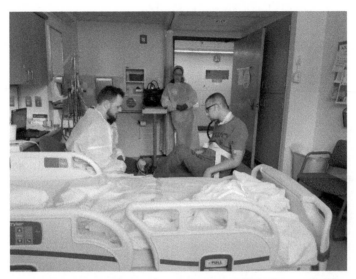

The day came that he was moved to the fifth floor. By then, we'd made friends with several nurses, aides, and sitters on the ninth floor. The sitters were still in place, and we were so thankful for that. We knew that soon they would replace sitters with a camera on a pole. Somewhere in that massive building was a room of people watching screens from cameras that were on poles in patients' rooms. They could speak to patients and guide them or give them directions. For instance, if a patient were to try to climb out of bed, the person watching could instruct them to stay in bed and ring the bell for the nurse to come help. They referred to this as the eye in the sky. We absolutely didn't want to go from a physical sitter in the room to an eye in the sky. We were very afraid he would fall if he tried to get out of bed unassisted. His brain still didn't tell his limbs what to do when and if a voice told him from the eye in the sky to get back in bed. We didn't know if he would understand that, let alone do it. He still had a long way to go. He couldn't walk yet without people on either side of him.

We got to the fifth floor. It was quiet! Like ICU. This was also a very old part of the hospital as far as the rooms went, so that was a little off-putting at first. But it turned into more of a cozy sort of place. He stayed there for an entire month! Often he would have heaches and want to lay his head on your shoulder.

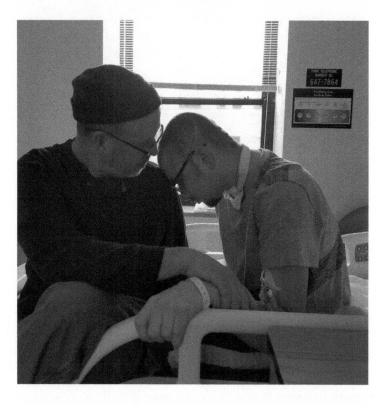

Each day he had physical, occupational, and speech therapies. He was learning how to rewire those blank spots in his brain. They did a lot of concentration games, word games, Lego kits, memory games. And he also had physical work with stairs—bending, stretching, and throwing balls. There were lots of people on the rehab floor, and he made a very good friend with a girl there who had been shot in a drive-by shooting. She was now paralyzed from the waist down. It was so sad. But they became good friends and would hang out together and play cards and watch TV.

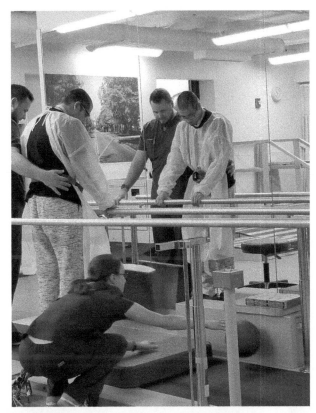

During this time, his boyfriend came less and less often. The writing was on the wall for everyone but Dawson. We were not sad that his boyfriend was on the way out the door. After all, he was one that Dawson would use drugs and drink with, steal things and sneak around with. Dawson needed better people in his life. It was interesting that not one other bad person he claimed as a friend ever came to see him. Not *one* of them came, sent a text, called, or sent a card. Not one reached out. Yet he still said they were his friends. He said they were afraid of us because we wouldn't let them visit. We reminded him that we let his boyfriend visit. He couldn't argue with that. We tried hard to help him understand that the people he had been hanging around with weren't friends at all.

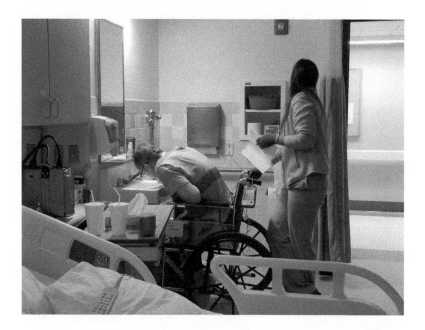

A month on the fifth floor made a difference in leaps and bounds with Dawson's recovery. They finally removed the feeding tube, and he learned to walk and didn't need the wheelchair anymore. We still assisted him with showering every night. I was really enjoying having dinner nightly with Dawson when I was there with him. We watched a lot of *Friends*, *The Office*, and movies when we shared a meal. I was reconnecting with Dawson on positive levels. I didn't know how much of conversations he was able to really understand, but I loved every minute of this time to bond with him and let go of the past. Tony also was enjoying his days with Dawson when he stayed there and I was back at home working. I'd stay a week at the hospital, then Tony would stay a week. Back and forth we went. Dawson was never alone at the hospital. Aunt Terri would take a weekend and give us a break when she could. It flowed very well.

Feeding tube removal.

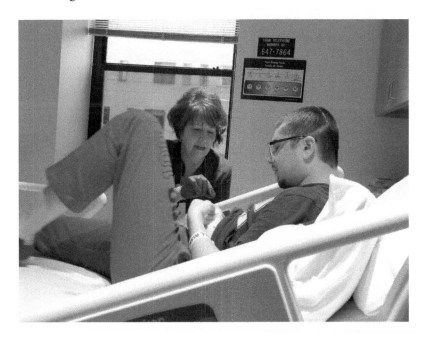

The hospital was anxious for Dawson to go to a step-down sort of a place and continue with rehab therapies. Finding a place for him proved to be one of the more difficult things to do. Many places were nursing homes, and that was not a place for a twenty-year-old. Or some were more of a hospital setting, and he didn't need that anymore either. Some places were a better fit but didn't take our insurance. Tony was a farmer, and so we had to pay for private insurance. Our deductible was really high, and it didn't cover a lot. We had paid and paid, trying to meet the deductible and out-of-pocket charges. And still, there was more money to be paid for things simply not covered.

Finally, we found a place in Carbondale, Illinois. It was six hours southwest from home. Before we made that long drive, the hospital let us take Dawson home for one day so that any family and friends that would like to see him before he would go spend a month in Carbondale could visit him. His boyfriend didn't call or come over. We hadn't heard from him for nearly a month by that time. Just a handful of our friends and family came. *None* of the people he said were his friends came. They all knew he'd be here, and as it was all over social media that could come see him. Not one called or showed up. Through this entire ordeal, Dawson had just two friends that were true friends. Sarah and Sydney. These girls had stuck by him and been loyal. They are true blessings in his life and also ours. They have continued to reach out and stay in touch. They are a support for him that can never be replaced.

On March 1, we packed him up at the hospital and went to say goodbye to everyone in ICU. There were hugs and tears and wishes of good luck. Then we drove for hours to get to Carbondale. They had three group homes for the clients, and each day, the clients were bussed to the facility where they had PT, OT, and speech therapy. They had a big screen TV, activities, and a lunchroom. They had some therapists there the clients met with a couple times a week. Looking back, it was not the right fit for him. And it burned up the last thirty days of inpatient rehab he could have had for a year. The fifth floor at the hospital burned up the first thirty days.

CHAPTER 4

The group houses the clients stayed in were in poor repair. They had both men and women in them. Some of the clients were wheelchair-bound, and some had such severe injuries; they had violent outbursts. Some didn't speak at all. Some rocked back and forth in a chair or wandered aimlessly and constantly around the houses and throughout the day facility. The staff members of these houses were just people off the street with no specific training. They really didn't have a lot of interest in the clients. They were just getting a paycheck. The rooms were dingy and old. The beds were ancient hospital beds or ones that looked like they were pulled from dumpsters. We didn't want to leave him there, but he needed help we couldn't provide at home.

There were house nurses that would go from house to house and pass meds and also a manager for each house. They didn't appear to be invested with the clients. It seemed more of a bother to them to do their jobs. Leaving him there that first night and going to the hotel was horrible. I was crying and at my wits' end. What were we doing? How could we leave him here in this place, with these people that seemed so indifferent? Dawson, even with his brain injury, was so much further along than nearly everyone else there. We didn't think they could help with what he needed help with. The next day, we went to the facility, and he was there with the other people, doing activities. We met with a caseworker to discuss what happened there and what to expect. We then went to the eating area and sat down with Dawson. He asked Tony if he had his license with him.

"Yes. Why do you ask?"

"Well, I wish I had mine so I could go to the gas station and get cigarettes. The nurse gave me a cigarette last night."

I came *unglued*! I was yelling immediately. Who gave my kid, with a brain injury, a cigarette! I was ready to pack him up and take him home that moment. I was so angry I left the room. The case manager talked to Dawson and Tony. Tony was angry with Dawson for smoking, and so was I. What was he thinking, smoking when he had a brain injury? Depriving his injured brain of oxygen! We nearly took him home that very day. The case manager reprimanded the nurse, and Dawson was moved into a different house. There were only three guys there, but one of them was there as an alternative to jail. I didn't know if that guy had a brain injury or not, but I didn't trust him at all. The house reeked of cleaning products and not in a good way. The floors were sticky, and the kitchen was cheaply made, with broken handles on drawers and cabinet doors coming off the hinges. There was a big TV in the living room and outdoor furniture for them to sit on.

His room had a creaky old hospital bed and a dented-up dresser with a TV on it. A small nightstand with a shelf to hold his bathroom items. We unpacked his stuff for the second time there. He got out a framed picture of him and his boyfriend. He put it on the nightstand. He still thought his boyfriend was, in fact, his boyfriend. He was long gone. I had looked on his social media, and Dawson was the furthest thing from that kid's mind by then. It made me sad that Dawson was alone, but better alone than with that guy who had just used him for whatever Dawson would do for him or give him.

Then we had to leave. We had to drive six hours home and leave him in this place. We felt they could help him some, but not a lot. We knew we couldn't bring him home, and there was no place else for him to go at that time where he could get a lot of care and focus on healing in several different ways, with speech, occupational, and physical therapy. I still felt just sick about leaving him there. It wasn't at all what we expected. A few days later, Tony was able to go and spend two days with him while I was working.

Then the weekend came, and I went by myself while Tony worked. I drove six hours in a rainstorm. It was awful. But I finally got there. Dawson hugged me and hugged me. Both nights I took him to eat and took him back to my hotel, where he would shower. It was much nicer than the shower at the house. I took him to Ulta at the mall. He had a facial and haircut. They did a deep scalp treatment. Having half of your skull removed could cause dandruff to accumulate on your skull! Who knew! The ladies at Ulta were wonderful and patient. They had him looking great and even trimmed his beard and mustache. We did this three weekends in a row. Dawson felt so much better. His skin had been breaking out as well, probably from being in the hospital all that time and then all the different medications and soaps being used at the house. Then I had to leave him again and drive that six hours home.

The next weekend, Tony went and did the same things. Tony actually got a tattoo of the Traumatic Brain Injury ribbon on his arm! Tony was a man who said he would NEVER get a tattoo! So this was a pretty big deal for him to do. For whatever reason he felt compelled to do this. Also there was a tattoo parlor right across the road from the hotel!

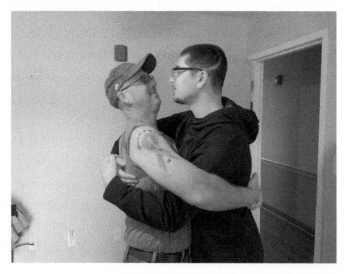

I think it was after that weekend that Dawson called and said he was so very sad and lonely. He missed us, his boyfriend, his grandparents, and Rachel. So he had stood in his room, banging his head against the wall! Oh my god! We freaked out.

"Get the house manager on the phone *now*!"

The manager got on the phone, and we questioned him. Did anyone check on Dawson? No. Well, this was what he was saying happened. Okay, they would have the nurse check him out. They would check on him every fifteen minutes for forty-eight hours and make sure he saw the counselor. I felt 100 percent helpless. I was heartbroken and so sad for him. I just wanted to hold my baby and rock him and fix him! The next weekend was the last weekend, and we went together to get him. That six-hour drive seemed endless. It was wonderful to pack him up and get him out of there. We had an exit meeting and were given prescriptions for occupational, speech, and physical therapy. We were also given a prescription for a wonderful thing called vocational rehab. They would do neurological testing to see where he was mentally and help with finding a suitable school and even go to college if he wanted to. We were quite excited to bring him home.

We drove to Tony's folks' house first. He was very happy to see them and talk for a little bit. Then we came home. While he had been gone all those months, I had time to make over his bedroom. I packed all his things in totes and stored them in the shed. I then cleaned, painted, and decorated the room.

He was happy to be here, and we were relieved to have him home finally. Now we could move forward, get him the therapies he needed, and move toward the future. The past, the bad people, the boyfriend—all were gone. He finally realized that his boyfriend had left him. When I was in Carbondale with him, he gave me the picture of the two of them and told me to burn it in the burn barrel at home. So I did. He was sad and also angry that his boyfriend had just stopped calling. It would take a long time and a lot of therapy for Dawson to let him go and move forward.

CHAPTER 5

Tony's friends decided they should have a benefit dinner for Dawson. So they started to plan it. I was taking Dawson for therapy and doctor appointments. Things were moving along. Rachel was still at school, but she was home frequently to visit, and she had some things to attend as the queen. So it was great to have her with us as well from time to time.

The day of the benefit was sunny and beautiful. It was early April. Soon, people started to show up. I had no idea how the benefit would turn out. Most of Tony's family came. There were many hugs. Some friends of Rachel's from school came, as well as a lot of my friends and Tony's as well. Friends we hadn't seen for years showed up! Dawson had two friends that were actually true friends. Sarah and Sydney. They have stood by him through everything. We trust them and treasure their friendship. People kept coming in the door or driving up for carry-out! The food was chicken and noodles, green beans and cookies. It was a community effort. Tony's friends made cookies by the dozens for this event, and others cooked all the food! It was amazing. I was so touched by the generosity and love these people were showing. The benefit raised $7,000! I was amazed and beyond thankful.

Things were truly looking up. I thought Dawson had surely hit his rock bottom, he was now ready to move forward and make better choices and find better friends. How could he not? He had been in trouble with the law for pot, but that had been dismissed because of the accident. He'd nearly died and was alive only because the ventilator was keeping him alive. He'd been to a neurological rehab facility, and now he was home. None of the bad people were around, and this was a fresh start. I could not have been more wrong.

We got him a new phone, and he was settling into a new routine. He was seeing a counselor, who told him to have alone time to reflect and think about his future and remember what the past had led him to. I was doing my CASA work, and Tony was in the field to plant. Rachel was at college, finishing her spring semester. One day, just a week or so after the benefit, Dawson asked if he could go for a walk through the neighborhood to have some alone time. I didn't like the idea at all. Would he be okay? Would he remember the streets? I said he could have twenty minutes. He had his phone. We had his old phone locked up. We kept it with all the things on it, in case we needed it for reference—his drug friends, pictures of him with pot and booze, horrible things he had written about us.

So I said, "Twenty minutes, and be back here." So off he went. He came back within the time frame, and the day went on. The next day, he wanted two of his girl friends to come over. I didn't like either one of them, as they had hidden him when he would sneak home from college. I knew they both had smoked dope with him in the past. Tony had a talk with both girls when they got here. He warned them that if anything happened, they'd be out of Dawson's life immediately. They came in and were hugging him and all excited. They all went to his room to watch TV. Then they came down and wanted to go on a walk. I was suspicious, but I let them go. What could I do, really? He was a twenty-year-old man. He'd been through hell. Surely, he wouldn't screw it up now. They weren't gone long. They got back, and the girls left.

The next day, I was sitting on the couch, making phone calls, and doing my CASA work. I started hearing a clicking sound when I was talking to a client on my phone. I knew right away it was a lighter. I got off the phone and listened some more. The floor grate in his room was almost directly above the couch. There it was again, clicking. My heart started to race; my skin felt hot. I knew without a doubt that he was smoking pot. I quietly put my laptop down and kept my phone in my hand. Then I ran up the stairs and into his room. He was lying on the bed, and the screen to the window was lying on the floor, as if the smoke and the stench would just drift out the window! He had his hand in his pocket.

I screamed at him, "WHERE IS IT!"

He immediately played stupid, which infuriated me even more. I grabbed his arm to yank it out of his pocket, and he resisted. I called Tony and yelled at him to get home *now*, that I had just caught Dawson getting high in his bedroom. I think at that moment, I was more angry than I had ever been in my life. After all he had been through, nearly dying and all that time in the hospital and then in Illinois and all he put us through and the community that had just gifted him all that money, he did *this*! After we had spent to get him all the help we possibly could, he was going right back to drugs! *How* could this be happening!

I was beyond angry with him. I just started yelling and saying whatever came to mind. It was truly horrible. Tony got home, and the yelling got louder. Dawson got angry then, which made it even worse. Things were said that could not be taken back. I started throwing clothes into a suitcase. I was done! I was going to take off and go stay in a hotel somewhere. I didn't even know where I would go, but I was finished! We called the therapist on her private number, and she talked us down. It took a long time, but she finally convinced me not to leave. It was one of the worst nights I can recall—worse in a different way than the accident. This was Dawson making the choice to use pot, even after all he had been through. This was me giving up. I felt I had truly failed as a mother, wife, just everything.

We then had to be with him 24/7. We took the phone and laptop. But we didn't know he was still contacting people on the old computer in his room. He had gone right back to manipulating, lying, and hiding things. It was tense in our house. Life was not peaceful. He had neurological testing to be done in Mishawalka; counseling, physical, occupational, and speech therapies were to be done at another hospital out of town. It took a lot of time and logged many miles. And all the while, the hurt feelings and knowing we couldn't trust him to be out of our sight kept us in a constant state of anxiety. We finally figured out he was contacting people using the old computer, so we took that away too. Each time a little trust was built or I could hug him without wanting to shove him away from me, something else would happen.

He'd go with Tony to the farm sometimes. Eventually, Dawson convinced Tony to let him stay with Grandma while he farmed. Then he would get on her computer when she took a nap, so no more going to the farm. We got him a volunteer job at the local animal shelter. There were no electronics he could get ahold of there. He enjoyed it and got to be with cats and dogs. We got a bit of a break as well.

We were really looking into getting him some help with his addictive personality. The doctors agreed that he would benefit from that. So I contacted the place my dear friend Tara told me about. It was called Capstone Treatment Center, way down in Arkansas. It sounded like a perfect place for him to go—except for the $70,000 price tag. Tony and I talked about it and called there many times. Finally, in July, we flew down there to check it out. Dawson was under lock and key with grandparents and strict instructions. We toured Capstone and talked to the director there. With Dawson's brain injury, we simply didn't know if it would work. They weren't sure either. They said they would try, and if Dawson couldn't grasp the program, they would let us know immediately. We flew home and discussed it with Dawson.

Capstone was very unique. They treated boys with problems with addiction to video gaming, pornography, drugs, alcohol, depression, anxiety, social disorder issues, and trauma of any kind. Part of their program included giving each client a Labrador puppy when they arrive. The guys are expected to take care of their pup and spend time with their pup every day. That was a big draw to get the guys to go there. Dawson was very excited about this and agreed to go. I don't know if he understood that we wanted him to go there because of the marijuana and to dig deep into his personal traumas to discover why he made the choices he did, but he agreed to go. I remember walking around my yard, thinking all these things over, thinking of all we had been through and what might be coming. I noticed the dandelions and recalled him saying he wanted to be the best dandelion picker ever. His innocent little face, with those big blue eyes . . .

My heart broke again, and tears ran down my face. *It's not supposed to be this way*, was all I could think.

He should be heading into his junior year of college, yet he'd flunked out in his freshman year. I was so sad and frustrated. My heart literally ached. Talking to Tony only brought arguments. We couldn't agree on anything about any of it. Rachel had checked out completely. She was working and spending all her extra time in Indy with her boyfriend. She didn't want to be around Dawson, and she didn't want to discuss any of it. My family was disintegrating. I didn't want to share the mess with any of my friends really. Maybe parts of it, but not all of it. Who wanted to tell anyone their son was becoming a drug addict and flunked out of college and ran away from home and lies to everyone?

It was never what I thought life would be like for my son. I knew how he got there. I understood exactly why Dawson was the way he was and how he got there from bullying and unhealed hurts. I just didn't know how to help him. His life had been filled with being made fun of by other kids, ignored by teachers, shunned by the few clubs he did join. I thought I was doing a good job with pep talks and understanding. When he came out to me, I did nothing but support and love him. Tony went to the school so many times when he was treated badly. Rachel stood up for him too. It just wasn't enough. He was so broken. But I was still filled with anger and frustration. I needed counseling to help me figure all these feelings out. I was able to speak to a counselor over the phone a few times, but her advice was to do some deep breathing, go for walks, and sign up for yoga! As if that would just fix it all!

August came. Rachel left for school, and the next day, Tony and Dawson flew to Arkansas. It wasn't necessary for both of us to fly down to drop him off. With the huge cost to send him there, there was no sense in paying for a third airline ticket. Suddenly, the house was quiet. No one was home but the cats and me. I walked into empty bedrooms. I sat down on Dawson's bed and sobbed. I couldn't stop. I cried with pain and utter anguish over all that had happened and was happening now and over the fear of what the future would bring.

When I thought I couldn't cry anymore, I stumbled into Rachel's empty room. She was gone again for school. She wouldn't be back until Thanksgiving, she told us. I lay on her bed and cried for all the pain she was going through and then for how much I missed her. My eyes were swollen and red. My vision was blurry. I walked into my bedroom. I saw a picture of the kids on my dresser from when they were little. They were sitting on a hotel bed next to my mom when she had come to visit us. They were so young and innocent. The big smiles on their faces to see Grandma Dorothy were precious. Both my parents had passed away when the kids were just six and seven years old. I was relieved my mom couldn't see Dawson now and all the choices and decisions he had made, but I sure could have used a hug from them. I cried until I drifted off to sleep. I felt completely empty and lost. This seemed to be an unending nightmare from which there was no escape.

Tony came home from Capstone, and we had many conversations. Sometimes we argued, and sometimes we agreed. Part of the program was weekly hour-long phone calls with Dawson's direct therapist. We also would get a twenty-minute phone call once a week from Dawson. The calls were at once inspiring and worrisome.

Was he getting the help he needed? Could he comprehend the program with his frontal lobe injury? Could he really understand what his choices and decisions had done to his body, mind, and spirit? Did he know how he had hurt us and Rachel to the point that Rachel had turned her back on him and barely spoke to us? Did he know how the extended family and friends were hurt and angry with him? Only time would tell.

One week he would seem to get it, and the next, he was back to square one. We were praying and trying to keep the faith here. I talked to Rachel at times, not wanting to push her or beg her to try to understand. She needed to do this in her own time. My heart hurt for her. I understood her anger. Tony began the season of harvest. I dug in with my CASA work. I also took this time of Dawson being away to take a creative writing program online. One of my assignments was to write a story from my perspective and then again from the perspective of another character in the story. I decided to write about Dawson's accident and then from what I could only guess was his perspective.

My professor wrote back and said this story moved her to tears, and she asked me to write more about it. So this is what I have been doing. It has been painful and brought released anger back at moments. Disappointment and sadness have touched me once again through writing. It has also been cathartic and helped me to heal. This story has not ended and maybe never will.

In October, Tony and I traveled to Arkansas for a family week at Capstone. He had to leave the field during harvest. This was a very big deal, as during harvest, it was all hands on deck are mandatory to get the crops in before winter. But we had to go. I was angry that once again, we had to sacrifice our jobs and lives because of the choices Dawson had made. I went into a family week, ready to let that kid have it with both barrels and shame the hell out of him. The anger, frustration, and hurt were bubbling to the surface, and he was going to know *exactly* all he had done to himself, to us, to Rachel, to the family, to our friends, and to the community. The lies we felt we had to tell to cover up the facts of him using drugs, drinking, stealing, lying, and failing out of college to save ourselves from the humiliation and shame of it all had been eating away at me for months. Oh yes, I had a *lot* to say to Dawson.

I loved him underneath it all. He was my son, a child of God, my firstborn, my dandelion picker. But the stress we had been experiencing for so long due to Dawson's choices and all that he'd affected was going to be laid out for him, very clearly and deliberately. He was going to know just how much havoc he had brought to our family. Tony was of a very different sort of attitude. He had so much compassion for Dawson and was much calmer than I was. I was very thankful for that. Tony himself has had much trauma in his life. We all have, to one degree or another. Maybe as a mom, I had more anger. Maybe it was anger at myself for feeling I had failed Dawson somehow. I was comparing some of my own life failures to Dawson's decisions. He and I were quite similar on many levels. I wanted him to be happy and have a good life and not make some of the same mistakes I had.

We flew once again to Arkansas. The first day of the family week was called Big Monday. The founder of Capstone spent about eight hours talking to all the parents about everything that Capstone encompassed. I searched the faces in the room. There were parents from across the country. Even a mom and dad from Alaska! All of us had entrusted Capstone to help our sons find their way back to health. I started to feel very alone and very separate from everyone else in the room. None of the other boys had brain injuries in addition to their specific problems. We all had to introduce ourselves and say a little something about our son who was in the program. Tony tried to talk but got choked up and couldn't get the words out. So I spoke, clearly and directly. Many parents looked me straight in the eye, and I could tell that they truly felt sorry for Dawson and us. I felt their pain when they spoke and noticed similarities in many of the situations.

The emotions in the room were palpable. All of us were afraid, tense, nervous, and angry on many different levels. Lots of parents asked questions and interacted with Adrian, the director. I, on the other hand, completely shut down. I was becoming withdrawn and 100 percent negative about the entire program. I didn't feel as if they could or had been helping Dawson at all. We broke for lunch. I almost ran out of the room. I wasn't speaking to Tony by then. I was wallowing in self-pity and depression. I filled a plate with food from the buffet they had catered. I chose a table away from everyone else. I wanted to see if anyone would choose to sit by us. No one did. It furthered my belief that we were not part of this group. Not included.

I knew this was how Dawson felt about many of the guys in the program. We had been told he was pushed out of the group almost from the start. His frontal lobe injury prevents him from showing much emotion on his face. A *flat affect* is the term used. The other guys felt he wasn't engaging in the process. Also, being gay didn't help either. His endless TV and movie quotes further pushed him out of the group. He didn't like sports, and shooting hoops was a popular pastime at Capstone. The afternoon wore on. I tried to loosen up some and pay attention to all that was being said to us. By 4:00 p.m., I simply could not take in any more information. I was just staring at the clock, wanting to be done, anticipating the next day when we would see Dawson and meet his counselor face-to-face, thinking of all the things I was going to say to Dawson and all the questions I was going to ask.

I was still feeling defensive, and I wanted Dawson to understand just how much he had hurt us. It was hard for me to keep in mind that he was hurt and broken as well. I was being unfair, unjust, but I couldn't stop myself. That evening, we went to a restaurant to have a nice dinner and relax. We talked about the long day. I apologized to Tony for going off the deep end that morning and my attitude throughout the day. I knew it was my defense mechanism. If I shut everyone and everything out, I wouldn't have to face the realities of the situation and the changes we'd have to agree to and then enforce. I was so afraid of what was going to happen once Dawson finished his time at Capstone.

The next morning, we got ready and went down to the lobby for breakfast. There were a couple of other families there, but no one was interacting with anyone else. We had to be at Capstone at 8:00 a.m. We left and drove the ten minutes to the facility. Other parents were already there, and some pulled in after we did. Once we were all in a cozy sitting room, some counselors came and explained that the moms would be staying there, while all the dads went to another room. We were going to be given an hour here each morning to talk, get to know one another, pray, or do whatever made us comfortable.

The night before, I had prayed for guidance and for a voice. "Please help me to connect with some of these other moms who surely are hurting as much or even more than I am."

Very quickly, conversation began, and one mom started to talk about the Bible and God and promises and books we could all read.

We fell into a discussion about Capstone, our sons' stories, and other kids left at home. When that first hour was up, I was feeling a lot of support from these ladies, and I was giving them my support as well. A counselor came to get us all, to send us outside to see the boys. Many of the families live near enough to Capstone, to be able to visit on Sundays. You could go any Sunday for three hours. We were almost twelve hours away by car, and to fly down for a three-hour visit on a Sunday was just not feasible. So we hadn't seen Dawson since August 19. It was now October 15.

The dads were already with the boys, by the basketball hoop. I started walking toward the group. A tall young man, wearing a ball cap, was walking quickly toward me. It actually took me a few seconds to recognize that it was Dawson! He looked *so* good! He was nearly running to get to me and hugged me so tight I could barely breathe! It was quite emotional. Tony walked up to us, and we had kind of a group hug. It was all moving quickly, and we were all talking at once. Dawson was trying to tell us about everything that he was doing at Capstone, and we were telling him how much everyone at home was rooting for him.

Several of the boys were shooting baskets. Dawson watched for a few minutes and said he would never try to shoot a basket. He said he couldn't do it and didn't want to be embarrassed or made fun of. I looked at Tony and told him he should go show those boys how it was done! Tony said he hadn't played in years and didn't know if he could hit the basket anymore.

I nudged him and said, "Come on, show them how it's done!"

Many of them were making baskets and playing really well. But I thought it'd be cool if Tony joined in. So he turned his ball cap backward, walked over, grabbed the ball, and hit a three-point shot—nothing but net on the very first try! The parents who were watching yelled out a cheer! It was a great moment! He continued to play a little bit, and Dawson and I watched. I told Dawson that Dad was making him look good in front of the other boys. He didn't really think so, but it did in a subtle way.

After a while, the nine families split into two groups, and we went to a meeting room to have group therapy. This week would be about facing the past, working through the trauma of the situation, working through our own traumas from our pasts, and coming together to face the future as a united, positive family unit. The therapists met with the parents for counseling and then individual counseling as well. Then we had a lot of counseling that included our sons as well. We were given homework to do every night.

We had to make posters showing what life might be like in five years for our sons and families. One side of the poster was a wasteland, showing what it would be like if our sons continued on destructive paths. The other side, the promised land, depicted what life might be like if our sons turned it around and left their bad habits behind. It was interesting when we all shared them the next day that hardly any of the boys thought they would die if they continued on their dark paths, while almost all the parents predicted death for their son. It was intense, and many of us shed tears. The stories shared were heart-wrenching and heavy. We moms continued our bond each morning before therapy started. The dads were less deep! Tony said they talked about sports and work more than anything else. We moms started a group text and exchanged email addresses and phone numbers. We prayed and talked about our situations. We all connected on levels I didn't expect.

After having therapy with Taylor, our counselor, I looked deep into my heart and mind. I thought of all the trauma I had experienced in my life. Much of it was incredibly dark. I had let these experiences mold me and hold me back. And I realized I had used a lot of negative things as an excuse when I was afraid to try something new or take responsibility for parts of my life I didn't like. I prayed about it. Wednesday night while we were in the hotel, I made the decision to let all the negativity go. It was ridiculous and pathetic that I had taken all my trauma and let it control me. I was ashamed of using my traumas as excuses to grow and become a better person. Once I let it all go, I truly felt free. I smiled. I was happy. I was determined to work through the rest of the week and support Dawson, not attack him with all the anger of the past and what had happened. It was over. He was in the best place he could be to start healing. I was hopeful he understood the program and working on himself. I hoped he was being truthful finally and going to make the positive changes he needed to remain clean, stay clean, and move forward.

The rest of the week continued to be intense and cathartic. We met Dawson's yellow lab pup. He named him Joey Tribbiani after the character on *Friends*. Dawson is a serious *Friends* fan, as am I. Joey is a great dog, and loves Dawson unconditionally. All the parents were allowed to eat lunch and dinner with the boys every day while we were there. We had more counseling and homework to do as the week ended. When we left on Friday, we felt much lighter and more positive about the next steps.

A few weeks have passed since we visited Capstone. It is just two days from now that we will head to Arkansas for the last time to bring Dawson and Joey back. Many thoughts and emotions are at play, of course. Has Dawson really changed? Or is he just going to say what he thinks we want to hear? I think of the other parents picking up their sons this week as well. The other moms hold places in my heart, as we have had similar paths with our sons. We mothers of sons who have lost their way, sons we thought we did our best to raise yet chose paths that have nearly destroyed themselves and their families.

I often wonder if the other moms beat themselves up, asking over and over where they went wrong. Didn't we all tell our children they could come to us with anything? Didn't we tuck them in every night and read a story and kiss their foreheads? Didn't we all teach them that drugs, drinking, stealing, and lying were all bad things and not to do them? Didn't we all think our boys were okay and growing up well and healthy?

During the family week, we learned that our own experiences can be transferred to our children on one level or another or several levels without knowing it. I didn't know that. I thought the secrets of my life were firmly tucked away, far from view, best forgotten. Learn from my mistakes. Move forward. Be a great role model for the kid. That's what I told myself to do. I never realized that things I experienced, shaped me in certain ways. And I didn't know that my attitude towards specific things, or situations, could have such negative effects on my children. My heart hurts knowing that I caused some reactions and behaviors that would drive my son to such a dark side of life. Never having dealt with issues of my own past has guided my life in a way that hasn't been healthy or well lived. So many mistakes and wrong choices—maybe this is common.

When you're in the moment, you do whatever it takes to get through it. You might not face the situation in front of you and bury it away. But when you do that, you change. It might be subtle, so quiet that you don't even realize it. Your temper gets a little shorter. You start to face the world with a little more negativity and disappointment. You start to see things with cynicism and expect the worst out of everything. These changes are gradual, and you realize on some level that the dandelions aren't so bright anymore. Everything becomes a dull chore. As things happen to you growing up and into early adulthood, you continue to bury the hard things, and your attitude continues to harden. Little joys bring back the sun from time to time, but by then, the darkness is your normal. It's comfortable. It's felt to be deserved. On the outside, you can fake being happy, but on the inside, you feel you deserve all the badness of the world.

So life moves on, and then children enter. I really and truly believed that I went through every bad thing in my life so that I could help my own children to have happy lives, untouched by pain and disappointment. But I never knew that all my pain would be transferred to my precious children, leaving them with pieces of my own wreckage to work into their own lives. Had I known any of that, I would certainly have gone to long-term therapy and counseling to become healthy before even thinking of having children of my own.

But as life's disappointments continued to pummel me, I continued to believe I could just hide it all from everyone.

At some point, we must let our children make their own choices and decisions. I can't imagine any parent not wanting the very best for their child. Don't we all want them to have better and do better than we did? I can't think of any specific moment that influenced Dawson to make the choices to use drugs and drink. I believe it has been a huge conglomeration of things that were too much for him to bear. My sweet dandelion picker with the biggest heart and the grandest hugs didn't think he could come to us about the things that were hurting him. He chose to lie and hide it all. He knew some of my life stories. Perhaps he was trying to protect me and not burden me with his own problems. If he has learned through the program at Capstone how to address those many hurts, learn from them, let them go and move forward, there is nothing left that I can ask for.

I also believe there are parents in similar situations that are also struggling with some of the same issues I am. Please know, you aren't alone. It took me awhile, but eventually, I trusted in close friends. I spoke to a doctor and had some counseling. I prayed a lot and took a big step back from the eye of this storm to evaluate and prioritize. I know I will never give up on my son. Things are sometimes incredibly frustrating on this journey, but I know there is a higher purpose for every moment of it.

I know that Dawson will always have to choose to do better. It won't come naturally to him. The darkness has been his normal for a very long time. As his mom, I want to erase all those hurts of course. I can't. He is going to have to find his journey on his own. He needs to know that the light is there, waiting for him to walk into it. He survived the horrific car accident that surely should have claimed his short life. He has a purpose. He must find it. Choices, decisions, jobs, maybe college again. How much his brain injury might slow him down remains to be seen. He has come so far from a dead coma to walking, talking, and even driving again that the sky is the limit. He has to be the one to push himself, trust himself, show that others can trust him. He must make an effort to live his life in the sun. He has been learning to trust God, to pray, and to believe.

We brought Dawson and his dog Joey home from Arkansas the week before Thanksgiving. He was happy to be home and see the family. Another Thanksgiving with Grandma Ethel. A Christmas with us and Rachel was home too. On Christmas Eve, Dawson and I went to church. Tony had a pig in labor, so he didn't go. Rachel was at her boyfriend's house, so she didn't go either. Just Dawson and I went to the candlelight service. We had some stern words before we got there and frustration. But when the service began, we both knew it was exactly where we needed to be. The mood of the celebration filled my heart and Dawson reached for my hand. We sang the songs of Christmas Eve and I thanked God again for allowing Dawson to be alive.

December 28th arrived and Dawson turned 21. My thoughts were of this day last year. I didn't see him on his 20th birthday, because he was getting high and drinking with his friends. I tried not to focus on that and focus on the present. The next day was it. The first anniversary of the accident. I didn't know how I would feel. Or how he would feel. It turned out to be an ordinary day. A few times we'd mention that a year ago, right now, the accident happened. And a year ago right now, we were in a room in the ICU at South Bend Memorial Hospital. It wasn't what I thought the day would be. I'm so thankful that we are here to talk about it and not standing before a grave, putting down pointsettias. Only God's grace has prevented that from being the reality.

January first brought moving day. I had found a sober living home in Indianapolis. He was so excited to move. We packed his things in Tony's truck and off we went. Moving in went very well and meeting with the director Jamie was great. We took him and met Rachel and Kyle for lunch. Leaving later in the day, things were positive and relaxed.

These stories really have no ending. Those of us who struggle and have hard lessons and rocky roads have to always choose to find the light, find the way, find the positive side. I hope that Dawson's story finds that light. Maybe one day, I will write more about his journey—a journey that is happy, positive, productive, and helpful to others who have been in the same kinds of darkness he has survived. If anything in this writing has helped you, its purpose has been fulfilled. May God bless you with life and light. My wish for you is that you find the high roads and that your journey is meaningful to you.

ACKNOWLEDGEMENTS

This story could not have been written without support from many. God has blessed me to share this story in hope that others may benefit from it. He placed just the right people in our lives, at just the right time to help all of us along this journey. Please never underestimate the power of God. He knows exactly why you are being faced with whatever the situation is that seems unsurmountable at the time. That being said, I would like to thank so many who have been supports from the very start.

First I would like to thank the person that called 911, because they were there when the accident happened.

First responders, ambulance and law enforcement. Thank you for getting Dawson to the hospital alive!

Pulaski Memorial Hospital ER staff. Dr. Healton specifically. Your heroic efforts saved Dawson's life and got him on the road to South Bend.

South Bend Memorial Hospital. Dr. Shaikah and all staff. ICU staff, Dan and Brittni. Sitters, nurses, aides, therapists. Bless you all forever!

Ronald McDonald House. Sue Losievski and staff. Bless you all SO much for taking care of us for 66 days. We love you!

Tony Ploss, my unwavering husband of 21 years. We are a united front in all of this and will continue on. We are learning to balance through it all.

Rachel Ploss. My daughter whom I could not possibly love any more than I do. Your incredible strength and resliance are breathtaking. I love you so.

Terri Sproles, my husband's sister, my sister in law. Terri has been a rock and a guide, helping from the moment she heard about the accident. She continues to be present and she and her family are a true blessing. We love you all so much.

Capstone Treatment Center. All you folks at Capstone are committed to serving each and every one of your clients with the very best help you can give them. Thank you for caring for our son and guiding him to a better way of life.

Jane Cornell. My 'sister'. Your prayers, texts and phone calls, have given me comfort for many years.

Sandy Crist. My dear friend who has always known how to make me laugh out loud! Your prayers and dinners are the best!

Cindy DeSabatine. You are SUCH a close friend. I love you dearly. You took such good care of me when I was home from South Bend. Shopping, lunches and pedicures helped keep the stress at bay!

Barbara DiLorenzo. My professor at NYIAD who said I should try to get this story published in the first place! Thank you for encouraging me to continue writing and find the way!

Deb Draper and Arizona crew! Thank you for nursing advice, love and prayers from across the country!

Jamie Engel. Circle City Sober Living director/owner. Thank you for taking on the guidance of Dawson as he steps forward into his journey.

Taylor Holsonback. Having you as Dawson's therapist at Capstone for three months was a true blessing. Thank you to infinity for helping and guiding him.

Dr. Eileen Hsu. A better pediatrician never lived! Your amazing care and love have blessed us to no end!

Sarah Farris. Thank you for being a TRUE friend and support to Dawson and to us.

Dr. Natalie Daily Federer. Your texts and hugs brought a lot of comfort.

Kyle Hettinger. Thank you for supporting Rachel and coming to the hospital every Friday.

Michelle Hettinger. Your gift of true friendship and caring for our animals when we had to be gone all the time was so very thoughtful.

Patty Hull. For Your prayers and becoming a friend in Christ, bless you.

Sara Kroft. The best boss EVER! Thank you for working with me, so I didn't have to leave my job. Thank you for being there, and for ALL the technical help!

Kara and Evan Richman, thank you for your support and love.

John Paul Owles. Thank you for believing in me and publishing Dawson's story. I am so very thankful you returned my first phone call to you!

Shelley Regensburg. My sweet cousin. Your continual prayers and staying in touch are a blessing.

Ethel Robinson. Great Grandma Ethel! What would any of us do without you!

Mashell Roudebush. My dear nurse friend! Sitting with Dawson for us while we went to the state fair pageant was such an incredible blessing. Thank you for being my friend.

Tara Terry. My dear friend! You told me about Capstone in the first place! Your endless support is amazing.

Deb Sheets. Never more than a phone call away! Your support is a true comfort.

Debbie and Steve Tennant. A family who's lives intertwined with ours. Prayers always.

Sydney Trippenfeldas. Thank you for being a true and loving friend to Dawson and the rest of our family.

Carol Winter. You're like a second mom to me. Your encouragement, mentoring, support and love mean so much to me.

I'd like to thank all those in my community that have supported us since Dawson's accident. Also friends who have continued to stay in touch and always ask how each of us are doing. Thank you to clergy who have had their congregations pray for Dawson's healing, everywhere from Indiana, to North Carolina, Arizona and Mexico! Every person we have met along this journey has touched our lives in a positive way. Some will be life long friends. Had Dawson's accident never happened, we would not know some of these amazing folks. Thank you all and God bless you.

ABOUT THE AUTHOR

Patricia Ploss is a devoted wife and mother residing in the picturesque state of Indiana alongside her loving husband, Tony. Together, they share the joys and challenges of parenthood, blessed with two remarkable children, Dawson and Rachel.

Patricia's journey as an author began with her deeply moving personal memoir, "The Dandelion Picker." This poignant account chronicles the harrowing aftermath of her son's near-fatal car accident and serves as a testament to the strength of the human spirit and the power of familial bonds. Patricia's raw and emotional storytelling in "The Dandelion Picker" touched the hearts of many readers and set the stage for her literary career.

Beyond her compelling writing, Patricia's life is enriched by a tapestry of passions. A voracious reader, she finds solace and inspiration within the pages of books, continually expanding her horizons. Her most beloved moments are spent with her family, cherishing the precious times they share together. Daily walks with their loyal canine companion, Joe, provide moments of tranquility and reflection, fostering her creativity and nurturing her connection to the world around her.

Patricia Ploss invites you to join her on a new literary adventure. Her words, infused with the wisdom and empathy gained from her life experiences, promise to captivate your heart and leave a lasting impression. Stay tuned for her upcoming work, as Patricia continues to weave tales that touch the soul and celebrate the profound beauty of human connection.

OTHER BOOKS BY PATRICIA PLOSS

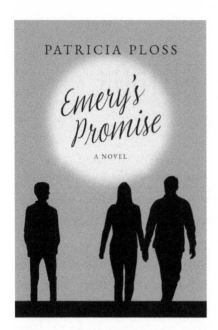

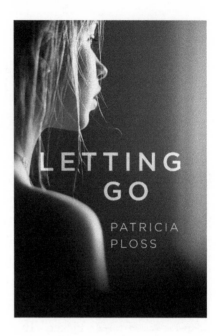

Emery Kincaid, independent realtor and recent widow, examines her life, determined to succeed and move forward, finds herself in an odd love triangle!

A dear family friend for years, Mark Stanton, is a long-time architect. His feelings for Emery have evolved from friendship to something more. As he slowly courts her, plans to change his own career develop, as his heart opens to new love.

Bart Moorhouse, born with a silver spoon in his mouth, has followed dark desires his whole life. Killing is not against his rules. When Emery pops up on his radar, he finds himself obsessed with her. The more Emery refuses to engage and indulge him, the more Bart is determined to have and control her.

Emery's determination to live might not be enough to save her from Bart's dark and violent will. Will Mark get there in time to stop Bart from his evil mission?

In 1962, seventeen-year-old Judy Bonner finds herself in love twenty-year-old Curtis Murphy. She also learns she is pregnant with his baby and due in June 1963!

Filled with fear, shame, and secrecy, Judy hides her pregnancy from her family for as long as she can! With no mother to turn to and only an angry, widowed father and an overbearing sister, Judy makes choices and decisions that only adults should have to make. Follow her story of love, trauma and letting go, in the early 1960s, where choices were few for girls who, "got in trouble!"

"Letting Go is close to home for me. As someone who was adopted as an infant in 1963, I know nearly nothing about my birth mother and her journey. Although I've searched for years, I've never been able to find her. This book is what I'd like to imagine her story was. My real parents are the ones who raised me. They've both been gone for many years now, but they will always and forever be my parents."

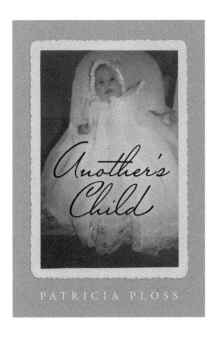

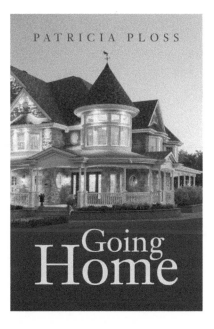

1961 brought the promise of a family to couple Tom and Dot Cornell. Until one day, several days past her due date, Dot nearly collapsed to the floor in excruciating pain.

Knowing something was horrifically wrong, Dorothy made her way to the couch and laid down. She hadn't felt her baby move in days. Everyone said that was normal, but she knew in her heart it was not!

Arriving home from work, her husband Tom found her out on the couch. She awakened to find herself in a pool of blood and they rushed to the hospital.

Was their baby dead? What had happened? Were they never meant to be parents? Emergency surgery would change their lives and their destiny to be parents.

Another's child might be their only way to become a mom and dad in the early 1960s.

Millie Parker found herself taking over her father's veterinary clinic when her dad retired, and he and wife Carolyn moved to Florida. Millie's life was on track, a profession she loved, established clientele, a great staff to work with, and old friends to reconnect with!

As she settled into her childhood home, pursuing her lifelong dream to follow in her father's footsteps, Millie expected to be happy!

Instead, she finds herself falling all over again for a high school crush! Now a widower with a young son, Al Alcoba seems further out of reach than in high school!

Running into Al and his son, Millie questions whether her life is really full! Would there be room in Al's life for another woman, since his wife had died? Would his ten-year-old son ever accept his dad having a new relationship?

Personal loss and the goal of helping others leads Millie down roads she never thought she'd travel.